Class War

The Jacobin series features short interrogations of politics, economics, and culture from a socialist perspective, as an avenue to radical political practice. The books offer critical analysis and engagement with the history and ideas of the Left in an accessible format.

The series is a collaboration between Verso Books and *Jacobin* magazine, which is published quarterly in print and online at jacobinmag.com.

Other titles in this series available from Verso Books:

The New Prophets of Capital by Nicole Aschoff
Playing the Whore by Melissa Gira Grant
Utopia or Bust by Benjamin Kunkel
Strike for America by Micah Uetricht

Class War
The Privatization of Childhood

MEGAN ERICKSON

VERSO

London • New York

First published by Verso 2015
© Megan Erickson 2015

All rights reserved

The moral rights of the author have been asserted

1 3 5 7 9 10 8 6 4 2

Verso
UK: 6 Meard Street, London W1F 0EG
US: 20 Jay Street, Suite 1010, Brooklyn, NY 11201
www.versobooks.com

Verso is the imprint of New Left Books

ISBN-13: 978-1-78168-948-6
eISBN-13: 978-1-78168-938-7(US)
eISBN-13: 978-1-78168-939-4 (UK)

British Library Cataloguing in Publication Data
A catalogue record for this book is available from the British Library

Library of Congress Cataloging-in-Publication Data
A catalog record for this book is available from the Library of Congress

Typeset in Monotype Fournier by Hewer Text UK Ltd, Edinburgh, Scotland
Printed in the US by Maple Press

CONTENTS

INTRODUCTION

The truth about baby shoes is that no one needs them. Newborns don't walk and they don't skateboard, but today's expectant parents can buy a miniature version of every niche adult shoe that's come to market in the past thirty years from Vans, Converse, Air Jordans, and Toms to shearling leopard print UGGs. Luxury retailer Stuart Weitzman offers gladiator sandals in gold leather with rhinestones in infant sizes for thirty-nine dollars a pair. J. Crew sells a tutu that costs more than the tasting menu at Jean Georges. The Bugaboo stroller—which is marketed as a "mobility concept" and is priced between $500 and $1,000 depending on the model—has become iconic baby "gear" after appearing in an episode of *Sex and the City*. In consumer culture, accessories are imbued with the power to express the personality of the owner or wearer, making us appear hip, countercultural, chic, nerdy, in on the joke, "socially conscious," etc.—but never has the demand to endow kids with an identity been higher. The luxury baby

market, which didn't exist before the 1990s, now brings in
$10.6 billion a year.[1]

As children grow, affluent parents continue to spend more
on learning experiences like sports lessons, country club
membership fees, enrichment CDs, trips to children's museums, and travel abroad.[2] They compete to secure coveted
spots in prestigious preschools—agonizing over whether to
include the "PhD" when addressing thank you notes to admissions directors.[3] It is not uncommon for a well-regarded
school on New York City's wealthy Upper East Side to receive
several hundred applications for ten or fifteen open seats, even
as tuition rises to be on par with that at private colleges.[4] New
York City's celebrated Dalton School, for example, offers a
well-rounded education in the humanities for $36,970 a year.

---

1   Jessica Grose, "The Luxury Market for Babies and Toddlers Is Back,"
Bloomberg, April 18, 2013, bloomberg.com; and Kelton Research, "New
Study Reveals Moms Feel Pressure to Buy Expensive Baby Brands, Even in
Down Economy," PRNewswire, January 31, 2012, available at storebrand-
formula.com.

2   Some of the spending is based on family values and preferences,
which I will discuss later (Chapter 4, especially on Annette Lareau's work),
but studies in the US and UK have shown that when low-income families get
additional cash, they increase spending on learning-related products and
activities: "For instance, in the New Hope anti-poverty experiment, families
used their additional income to enroll children in child care, after school
activities, and other enrichment programs." Neeraj Kaushal, Katherine
Magnuson, and Jane Waldfogel, "How Is Family Income Related to
Investments in Children's Learning?" (Paper presented at Project on Social
Inequality and Educational Disadvantage: New Evidence on How Families,
Neighborhoods and Labor Markets Affect Educational Opportunities for
American Children, Washington, DC, September 24–25, 2009), xteam.
brookings.edu/eoac.

3   Anastasia Rubis, "Kindergarten 101: A Wait-Listed Mom Confesses
All," *Observer*, April 8, 2002, observer.com.

4   Emily Jane Fox, "How New York's 1% Get Kids into Preschool,"
CNN, June 10, 2014, money.cnn.com.

New York magazine's guide to "Cracking the Kindergarten Code" provides painstaking answers to the questions, "Will bribery work?" and "Should you despair of getting Junior into an Ivy if he doesn't get into a top-tier kindergarten?"[5] Emily Glickman, a preschool admissions coach who helps urban parents navigate the application process—herself a graduate of the city's elite private schools and specialized public high schools—says that Bill Clinton is "a popular choice for recommendation letters" among families she works with.[6] The right private preschool is expected to open the door to admission to the right elementary, middle, and high school, then the Ivy League, and a lifetime of success.

Free public preschool or "Universal Pre-K" (UPK) is hardly easier to get into than private school. In 2013, the most popular programs admitted less than 5 percent of the families with four-year-olds who applied. In the 2014 school year, even after New York City mayor Bill de Blasio doubled the number of seats available to 40,000, only 62 percent of families who applied got a position.[7] And while middle-class moms and dads may not be buying $1,000 strollers, elite parents have reshaped mainstream cultural expectations. Nearly 40 percent of first-time mothers said, in a 2012 survey, they felt guilty for not being able to afford a specific product for their newborns.[8]

---

5   Andrew Marks, "Cracking the Kindergarten Code," *New York* magazine, November 28, 2005, nymag.com.

6   Eliza Shapiro, "Stuck in New York City Private School Wait List Hell," *The Daily Beast*, February 15, 2013, thedailybeast.com.

7   Pamela Wheaton, "Schools' Pre-K Almost Full; 38% Get No Seat," *Inside Schools*, June 5, 2014, insideschools.org.

8   Kelton Research, "New Study Reveals Moms Feel Pressure to Buy Expensive Baby Brands."

Meanwhile, nearly a third of American children live in households with incomes below 60 percent of the national median of about $31,000 (as of 2008).[9]

It is a stark contrast. Here's another: Only 5.3 percent of children in Norway, about 7 percent in Finland, and 10 percent in Denmark live in such extreme poverty. The wealthiest country in the world, the United States is slotted just above Mexico, Israel, Spain, Greece, and Latvia when it comes to the percentage of children living in impoverished households—behind thirty-five out of forty-one nations surveyed.

These families are not the audience for essays on "How to Parent Like a German." Most stories in that vein (and there are plenty—American expatriates writing on the wisdom of European parenting now constitutes an entire genre) focus on the internal battles of individual parents and use psychological language to admonish American parents to simply let go and relax, to back off, quit being a helicopter parent. Sara Zaske, an American mother and journalist, writes in *Time:* "The first time I went to a playground in Berlin, I freaked. All the German parents were huddled together, drinking coffee, not paying attention to their children who were hanging off a wooden dragon 20 feet above a sand pit. Where were the piles of soft padded foam? The liability notices? The personal injury lawyers?" Ultimately, she gains the confidence to let her child play freely on the playground and even

9   Gonzalo Fanjul, *Children of the Recession: The Impact of the Economic Crisis on Child Well-Being in Rich Countries, Innocenti Report Card 12* (Unicef, 2014), unicef-irc.org.

go to the store by herself. She's come to terms with the more laid-back style of German parents—and that is where her story ends.[10]

But of course, it's the beginning of a much more interesting question. American parents are not suffering from a collective delusion. The phenomenon they are responding to is real. *Why* are American parents of all classes experiencing such pressure to ensure that their children are constantly being giving every advantage—being constantly overseen and prepared for the competitive world of adulthood?

Pamela Druckerman, another American mother, and the author of *Bringing Up Bébé*— which is much more interesting than its cutesy title suggests—began writing her book after moving to France and observing that French babies start sleeping through the night at two or three months old, don't seem to require constant adult supervision, and are capable of hearing the word "no" without collapsing. "French parents are very concerned about their kids," she writes—but they aren't *panicked* about their child's well-being, or exhausted, as many Americans seem to be. Druckerman attributes the difference to widespread absorption in the problem of children "falling behind" since the 1990s, and to the growing sense that children are psychologically fragile. Though the rate of violent crime has fallen dramatically since the early 1990s, "news reports create the impression that children are at greater physical risk

---

10   Sara Zaske, "How to Parent Like a German," *Time*, February. 24, 2015, time.com.

than ever." She also points out the real economic advantages to being a parent in France: French parents have access to full-time, government-subsidized and regulated day care. Middle-class parents prefer crèches to hiring nannies privately. Druckerman recalls the different reactions she got from her American versus French friends and family to finding a place for her child in a crèche. Her mother paused tepidly over the phone. An American friend said she liked more individualized attention for her own child than a day care could provide. French friends, on the other hand, congratulated her, and "practically crack[ed] open champagne."

American ambivalence toward day care makes sense given the lack of federal oversight and regulation and the high turnover and low pay for teachers, which means program quality varies immensely. It also reflects a larger ambivalence about women's role in society: The so-called "mommy wars" are still going on here, as conservatives continue to question whether a woman's place isn't really at home with her kids. Additionally, there is a class stigma to day care in the States that does not exist in most European countries. Institutionalized day care in America has traditionally had a compensatory role—functioning as a way to make up for perceived deficits in low-income families, from early-twenti-eth-century programs aimed at working-class women to the first federally funded system of early childhood education and health care, Head Start, which was founded in the 1960s and means-tested, meaning only families making below a certain income level were welcome. Finally, and more subtly, day care is a collective and—in comparison to the private household—public space, requiring cooperation among large numbers of families, teachers, and administrators, in a country that above all values individual freedom. American families worry constantly that another child's needs will take precedent over the needs of their own child.

It is not out of the question that a child's needs will go unmet in the United States. In fact, it happens every day. And it's changing the way we understand what it means to be a child—to learn and grow.

For nineteenth-century Romantics, childhood was (at least idealistically) an innocent phase of life that transpired mostly outside of the economy when, as Wordsworth wrote, "every common sight" appears "apparell'd in celestial light."[11] These values persisted among middle-class Europeans and Americans well into the late nineteenth century. But, against a background of increasing wealth inequality, a shift has taken place. Today, childhood in America has come to be regarded in the mainstream as a period of intense preparation for the competitive pressures of adulthood.

Parents struggle to give their children the edge that they will need to survive in the stratified and competitive labor market. The nurturing and raising of children, once seen as deserving of fierce protection from market forces, has now become intertwined with economic pressures: It is never too early to start equipping a child with the skills and personality traits that will ensure productivity and success in the global

---

11 "Ode: Intimations of Immorality from Recollections of Early Childhood."

economy. This can lead to a focus on the outcomes of child-rearing, rather than the day-to-day pleasures, for both parent and child. The pressure to be more and more involved is endless and exhausting.

For the past three school years, I have worked as the administrator of a preschool and after-school program for the largest community organization in the country. Both programs are economically and racially diverse in a way I had not previously experienced working as a volunteer, mentor, and student teacher at three different public schools in New York City for a year and a half prior. One of my jobs is helping parents from all backgrounds apply to public and private kindergarten. Every year, the demands of wealthy parents and fears (and disappointments) of middle-class and lower-income families have intensified. During a workshop on kindergarten admissions, when discussing the student-centered, progressive education provided for free by some elementary schools that require an admissions exam or luck to get into, one middle-class parent raised her hand and asked, heartbreakingly, "Why don't all of the schools have that?"

Her frustration is understandable. While there is no single measure that automatically and uniformly creates a better learning environment, smaller class sizes have been consistently linked to higher student achievement.[12] Yet former New York City mayor Michael Bloomberg, one of several urban mayors including Rahm Emanuel of Chicago to have

---

12   Editorial Projects in Education Research Center, "Issues A–Z: Class Size," *Education Week*, July 1, 2011, edweek.org.

autocratic control over the city's public schools, said in December 2011[13] that his ideal education system would require firing half of the city's teachers and paying twice as much to the remainder to teach classes double the size. In New York City, public school class sizes rose for the third consecutive year in 2011.[14]

On the other hand, student-to-teacher ratios at the nation's elite private schools like Sidwell Friends, attended by President Obama's children, is one teacher for every ten students in the lower grades, with class sizes of four-teen to sixteen students in the upper school, permitting "individual attention, group discussion, and close interaction between students and teachers." The curriculum is "experiential and small group based," and students learn through the use of manipulatives, models, games, and creative work. In the lower school, art is integrated into the classroom every day. Students have art class once a week and music class twice.

For the rest of the country, time spent on creative subjects like art and music has dropped precipitously. In a study on the effects of the No Child Left Behind Act, independent nonprofit Center on Education Policy (CEP) found that curriculum and instructional time had changed since the passing of the standards and accountability measures, with increased time for tested subjects (ELA and math) and

---

13 Mary Ann Giordano and Anna M. Phillips, "Mayor Hits Nerve in Remarks on Class Sizes and Teachers," *New York Times*, Dec. 2, 2011, nytimes.com.

14 Anna Phillips, "Class Sizes Grew Again, New City Figures Show," WNYC, Nov. 15, 2011, wnyc.org.

reduced time for other subjects (social studies, art, science, music, phys ed, and lunch and recess) since 2002. Both the increases in time for tested subjects and decreases in time for other subjects were more prevalent in districts with schools that were identified as in need of improvement.[15]

It's unclear to what extent hours spent in foreign language classes, art classes, or recess inside and outside of school actually produce the outcomes affluent parents seek—an increase in IQ and other standardized test scores, a competitive edge among their peers. In fact, in their essential and foundational research, the Marxist sociologists Samuel Bowles and Herbert Gintis document that "social class or racial differences in IQ are nearly irrelevant to the process of intergenerational status transmission," a strong critique of well-meaning liberal projects (like the early childhood and health program Head Start) to bring about equality by making access to educational opportunity more equitable.

What is clear is that family wealth and children's academic achievement are related, well before children enter school. An overall $3,000 increase in family income is correlated to higher academic achievement equivalent to two extra months of schooling.[16] And families spend more money on enrichment items for children as their overall expenditures (a proxy of income) rise.

15   Jennifer McMurrer, *NCLB Year 5: Choices, Changes, and Challenges: Curriculum and Instruction in the NCLB Era* (Washington, DC: Center on Education Policy, 2007).

16   Greg J. Duncan, Pamela A. Morris, and Chris Rodrigues, "Does Money Really Matter? Estimating Impacts of Family Income on Young Children's Achievement with Data from Random-Assignment Experiments," *Developmental Psychology* 47, No. 5 (September 2011): 1263–79, ncbi.nlm.nih.gov.

This is true within specific families as well as a trend over time.[17] Spending on child-enrichment goods and services has jumped for families in the top quintiles to a far greater extent than for those in the bottom income quintiles, beginning in the 1970s and intensifying by 2005, according to four expansive consumer expenditure surveys conducted between the early 1970s and 2005 to 2006.[18] High-income families are more likely to move to have better access to resources for their children, both outside of school as well as within it, because the United States relies heavily on property taxes to fund education, meaning that housing policy has deep consequences for the distribution of and access to educational resources.[19]

What is at stake when some children go to school hungry, and others go to school in $1,000 strollers? When rich kids get recess and art class, and poor and middle-class kids don't?

When a new parent buys a pair of shoes for his baby that some grown women will never be able to afford, or enrolls her toddler in a Mandarin class with the intent of making the child a more desirable hire—or spends hours painstakingly preparing kindergarten applications with the help of a hired

---

17 Kaushal, Magnuson, and Waldfogel, "How Is Family Income Related to Investments in Children's Learning?"

18 Ibid., and Duncan, Morris, and Rodrigues, "Does Money Really Matter?"

19 "Property wealth varies significantly between districts within a state. As a result, districts with small property tax bases typically find it harder than those with large property tax bases to generate local revenue for schools. Compounding the problem, districts with more-costly-to-educate young-sters are often not the ones with the large property tax bases." National Research Council, *Equity and Adequacy in Education Finance: Issues and Perspectives* (Washington, DC: National Academies Press, 1999). See also Kathy Checkley, "Money Matters: A Primer on K–12 School Funding," Center for Public Education, July 2, 2008, centerforpubliceducation.org.

consultant—what exactly is being bought, and what is being
sold? The strollers and cashmere blankets and Baby Mozart
CDs are but signifiers of a broader economic trend. At the
same time that educational mobility has decreased, meaning
economic advantage and disadvantage is being passed along
the generations in America, the economic struggles of low-
income and working-class families have visibly increased. It
is as hard as it has ever been to be poor in America, and
getting harder. It's also getting harder to hold onto being
middle class. Anxiety among even the wealthiest parents is
not unfounded, given the increasing economic stratification
even within the top 1 percent of the country's earners.

The increasing pressure reported in popular parenting
books and magazine articles since the 1980s and 1990s corresponds exactly to the intensification of wealth concentration
and competitive economic pressure on American workers. If,
in a society organized around a free market economy, we aim
to above all buy cheap and sell dear, it is in the interest of an
employer to pay workers as little as possible—indeed, he
must, to keep up with the others, so that globalization is
described even by the *Economist* as one long race to the
bottom.[20] Mainstream economists routinely observe that the
deep and wide-ranging drop in labor rights in the 1980s and
1990s is due to competition for foreign direct investment.[21] As
worker protections slip and competition for jobs intensifies,

20   C. W., "Racing to the Bottom," *Free Exchange* (blog), *Economist*,
November 27, 2013, economist.com.
21   Ronald B. Davies and Krishna Chaitanya Vadlamannati, "A Race to
the Bottom in Labor Standards? An Empirical Investigation," *Journal of
Development Economics* 103 (July 2013): 1–14, sciencedirect.com.

"degree inflation" occurs, meaning jobs that once did not require a credential now do, "pushing the less educated even further down," as the *New York Times* noted in 2013,[22] when the unemployment rate for workers with no more than a high school diploma was more than twice that for those with a bachelor's degree. Of course, it's not the degree alone that matters—it's a sorting mechanism for dividing "good" workers from "bad." "College workers are just more career-oriented," one managing partner at a law firm told the *Times*, summarizing the conventional recruiter wisdom. "Going to college means they are making a real commitment to their futures. They're not just looking for a paycheck." Conventional wisdom aside, the result is racial discrimination and the reinforcement of social class: Today a white high school dropout has the same chance of getting a job as a Black college dropout. Black students must complete two additional levels of education above their white peers to have the same probability of getting a job.[23]

Many American parents have understandably come to view education as a process of ensuring one's child has met every milestone on time or early. K–12 schools are increasingly responsible for providing this kind of education,

---

22 Catherine Rampell, "It Takes a B.A. to Find a Job as a File Clerk," *New York Times*, February 19, 2013, nytimes.com.

23 Abigail Bessler, "A Black College Student Has the Same Chances of Getting a Job as a White High School Dropout," *ThinkProgress*, June 25, 2014, thinkprogress.org. The best extended discussion of this reality can be found in Jean Anyon's *Radical Possibilities: Public Policy, Urban Education, and a New Social Movement* (New York: Routledge, 2005), which is sadly still relevant a decade after its initial publication, even though some of the statistics and patterns have changed.

whether that means assisting wealthy parents in their goals for their children's achievement or compensating for what is seen as working-class parents' inability to provide these opportunities for their children.

Wealthy and middle-class parents exercise an inordinate amount of power over the broad values and direction of the public and private school systems, whether that is directly, as philanthropists funding specific projects and visions for schools, or simply because they have more time and say in a society where they are more able to make their voices heard.

A subtle transformation of what we expect from schools is underway, that corresponds to the increasing burdens placed on parents for securing the futures of their individual children, with greater emphasis placed on testing and the STEM (science, technology, engineering, and math) subjects, rather than critical thinking. The French philosopher Louis Althusser imagined schools as a place of direct indoctrination into the values of the most privileged and powerful members of society. Bowles and Gintis present a far less mechanistic, and more complex, picture of schooling's place in society. They see schools as integrated into the social and economic system, and a place where youth are socialized into the discipline and disempowerment of the American workplace, and where a specific set of values is cultivated in students through relationships with peers, teachers, and administrators depending on what class they are from. Upper-middle-class kids may be encouraged to be articulate, self-confident, and to negotiate with adults, all personality traits that are required from supervisory, white-collar jobs, whereas lower-middle-class and working-class kids may receive subtle cues that they should respect authority and become subordinate. This is true in my own experience of the American education system. Adults complain about the inconvenience and anxiety of getting past airport security. Think about what it means to pass through a metal detector on your way to school every day, as 100,000 New York City public school students do.[24] When entry to class feels more like entry into a foreign country, complete with checkpoints and armed police officers, the message is clear: This space is not yours. You don't own it; you are merely passing through. And the fact that metal detectors are also essential components of the American criminal justice system does not escape students.

In a 2015 Change.org petition with one hundred signatories, a New York City public school student writes,

The majority of students New York City schools are Black and Latino. Metal detectors in schools contribute to the idea that Black and Latino teenagers should be treated like criminals. When passing through metal detectors students feel hassled, uncomfortable, annoyed, and that their rights are being violated. Metal detectors in schools break the connection between students, teachers, and school administrators and contribute to a distrust of authority.[25]

---

24 A large majority of NYC school students who pass through metal detectors on a daily basis on their way to school are Black and Latino (82 percent of students, while Black and Latino students compose only about 70 percent of New York City's student population). This will be discussed more fully in Chapter 1.

25 "Put an End to Metal Detectors in Public Schools," change.org.

The word "distrust" is important. For at the same time that the school experience is shaping students, students are shaping the school. Working-class students and students of color actively *resist* the implication that they are "like criminals." Likewise, some school staff from teachers to paraprofessionals and even school safety officials question the authority of administrators and the messages being handed down implicitly and explicitly to students. For example, one of the teachers I interviewed, Brooke Carey, described working at a public school in Sheepshead Bay, which served predominantly low-income students of color and had been repeatedly labeled "failing" by the time she started working there.

> They had a stupid policy where kids weren't allowed to wear hats or do-rags. And you know, it would be so anxiety-inducing for me, because clearly I didn't really care. If he was in my class or she was in my class and she was doing her work and she was sitting there and collaborating and whatever else I need her to do, a hat did not matter to me. But they sort of picked on these ridiculous rules, in my mind, that then became an opportunity to confront the kids. So you'd see the dean or an administrator just walking, peering through classroom walls, almost like a gotcha. And the stupid [rules about student cell] phones. It was just—why are we going to create this confrontational environment with the students when there are larger issues?

Carey refuses to "write kids up" for breaking superficial rules that promote a punitive environment. On a structural level, schools may replicate and perpetuate the inequalities that occur in society, but they are also made up of real people, working together every day, and that is a powerful realization.

As a volunteer "mentor" at Chinatown's Urban Assembly Academy of Government and Law, which serves primarily low-income students of color, I taught a civics class on the Civil Rights Movement and grassroots organizing. The idea was that students would choose an issue that they saw in their community and build an action plan to solve it. The program was meant to help struggling teachers in struggling schools connect with and "empower" their students. What I gleaned from examples in other schools was that students were encouraged to do community service projects like picking up trash around their neighborhood, or writing letters to elected officials about the injustices of the American penal system. When I talked about what kind of project we should work on and things I'd done with other classes in the past, the tenth-grade homeroom class of all boys surprised me by bringing up the issue of student representation. They felt powerless over their own day-to-day lives, due to, among other things, high teacher turnover and a principal who didn't listen to them (and who I would come to find was wildly unpopular with teachers as well). Over the next few months, we laid out a proposal and plans for a student government, which the teacher promised to help implement. Instead, as I discovered when I followed up with him, he quit teaching, leaving the school to go back to a job in finance.

In writing this book, I've drawn on my own observations

over the past five years working with kids from birth through twelfth grade in New York City—the nation's largest school district, serving over 1 million children each year—in a variety of public schools and community-based organizations. I spent the 2014–15 school year touring and observing public and private schools all around the city, and interviewing public and private school teachers, all of whom had had at least three years and two of whom had had ten years or more of experience. New York City is an interesting case study, because, along with Chicago, its standards for children as well as the overall politics and policy of education reform (the history of which you will find in Chapter 2) are indicative of what is going on in many public school districts, particularly urban districts, around the country. Education reformers in New York City are among the most prominent in the country.

In New York City, as in America, children are poorer than ever. They spend their days in highly unequal schools in thrall to philanthrocapitalists who hope to see the American education system become more like corporations, with teachers and students accountable for showing measurable yearly progress in meeting education goals, which are narrowly defined as improving scores on standardized math and reading tests. Despite being seen as a "great equalizer," the American education system often perpetuates or does nothing to mitigate deepening class inequities.

But that does not mean that the massive and inspiring project of public schooling should be abandoned. Inequality does not begin or end at school. The idea that schooling creates it, or that schooling can put an end to it is a fantasy embraced by liberal and conservative thinkers and politicians alike. Still, public schools are where about 50 million of America's 75 million children spend their day: 89 percent of school-aged children attend public K–12 schools, and about 1.3 million children attend public pre-K. Public schools employ 3.1 million full-time teachers, and many more substitute teachers, paraprofessionals, cafeteria workers, and bus drivers. The philosophy that governs our schools is intimately connected to the philosophy that prevails over our workplaces—the two dominant environments of civic society—since American workers use schools as child care, and since school children will one day grow into adults. Conditions and rights in schools are thus of consequence to every single American, worker and nonworker alike, parent and nonparent.

When I think about what role schools should serve, I think about a conversation I have constantly with parents whose children are enrolled in the day care I oversee. Sometimes, around the age of three, children who have formerly woken up every day and gotten dressed and eaten breakfast eager to come to school will start crying every morning and telling their parents that they don't want to go. Parents always respond with concern, and sometimes even consider withdrawing their children, only to then have their children beg them tearfully to let them stay. My response is, "Do you always feel like getting out of bed in the morning and going to work?" The answer is, of course not. But we go.

We go because we need to make money to pay rent or a

mortgage and to feed our families and ourselves. We go, because we know that sometimes, even when we'd rather sit on the couch all day and relax, the joys of getting up and leaving the house to interact with others ultimately outweigh the immediate impulse to wrap oneself up in a blanket and watch reruns of television shows. As adults, we have a perspective based on experience and the ability to regulate our own behavior that young children lack. These are positive, social impulses that lead to a functioning society, impulses which we rightly want to pass on to our children.

The problem of a hypercompetitive society organized around the free market is that people don't just work to be social and to ensure the basic needs of all are met fairly and equally. They work in the service of an alienating and inhumane economic and political system that allows billionaires to hoard resources while nearly a third of American children live in poverty. This is what must be dismantled, not public education.

One day at school, I was building with blocks with a little girl and a little boy. We were absorbed in what we were doing, constructing roads and bridges and towers. The little girl suggested we build an airplane. But how would we do that, with only rectangle and square blocks? Excitedly, the little boy found some long, thin, cylinder-shaped blocks, and showed us how they could be wings. Then, the teacher announced it was time to clean up. I fought the impulse to keep building. The little girl looked up at me with wide eyes and a sadness that seemed, to me, quite adult. "I don't want to stop playing," she said, not in a whine, but with the sincerity and gravity an adult might use to talk about death or the passing of time.

I had a few choices at that moment and ran them over quickly in my head. Each involved placing a particular value on the individual in relation to the group, and play versus the work of cleaning up. All of the other children were cleaning up, so that they could move on to the next large group activity, and if we continued playing, they would sit, bored, waiting for us to finish. I did not want to teach the girl that her own needs took precedence over the group's. But I also did not want to teach the girl that cleaning up and listening to the rules takes precedence over playing, experimenting, and controlling your own environment. I said, "I don't want to clean up either! I'm excited, and I don't like being stopped in the middle of what I'm doing. Let's ask if we can finish what we're doing, and then clean up." We negotiated with the teacher for a few more minutes, then joined the rest of the group.

I believe that American schools and workplaces must be transformed to integrate the human love of play—making meaning through building with blocks, experimenting with words, listening to music, dancing. I don't mean that play should become part of daily life for the sake of increasing working productivity, the way tech startups put ping-pong tables and ball pits on their "campuses" to encourage workers to stay in the office longer and longer. I mean that what we understand as work should be revised and restructured around both basic human needs (like caring for friends and family) and complex needs, like being creative—instead of around the relentless drive for profit. Of course, there are some jobs that are unpleasant for the individual but will always need doing, for survival, even in a more humane society than we have at present. Those tasks should be undertaken by everyone, equitably.

Those are my values, and they influence the way I conduct myself at school every day. Even the simplest exchange between adults and children reflects fundamental beliefs about how we should behave toward each other and ourselves, and how we should live. When teachers, parents, and students fight for control over their own schools, they are fighting for a say in how schooling is defined: What is the "work" of a child or an adult? What should it be? That is the subject of this book.

1

PUBLIC SCHOOLING: WHO LISTENS? WHO SPEAKS?

Every time I see a young person who has come through the system to a stage where he could profit from the system and identify with it, but who identifies more with the struggle of Black people who have not had his chance, every time I find such a person I take new hope. I feel new life as a result.

—Ella Baker

The paradox of education is precisely this—that as one begins to become conscious, one begins to examine the society in which one is being educated. The purpose of education, finally, is to create in a person the ability to look at the world for oneself, to make one's own decisions, to say to oneself this is black or white, to decide for oneself whether there is a God in heaven, or not. To ask questions of the universe, and then to learn to live with those questions, is the way one achieves one's own identity. But no society is really anxious to have that kind of person around. What

societies really ideally want is a citizenry which will simply
obey the rules of society.   *—James Baldwin, 1988*

When the odds are against you, how can you prosper?
When during childhood you become a man
And after that derange into a monster
This is for all my misunderstood brothers
Who won't settle for minimum wages
Who are a danger to themselves and others
For all the carnales confined up in cages.
            —Alejandro G. Vera, from Push and Pull: Poetry by
                    Residents of the Cyndi Taylor Krier Juvenile
                            Correctional Treatment Center in
                                    San Antonio, Texas

Students are admitted to Stuyvesant, an elite public high
school in New York City where I worked as a student
teacher of ninth-grade English, based solely on their performance on a single entrance exam. To receive a spot at the
school, they must score in the ninety-ninth percentile on the
Specialized High School Admissions Test (SHSAT).
Stuyvesant is one of nine Selective High Schools overseen
by the New York City Department of Education (along
with Brooklyn Tech, Bronx Science, and the LaGuardia
High School of Music & Art and Performing Arts, "the
Fame school," which is alone among the other eight in
requiring a portfolio rather that exam results for entrance).
A quarter of Stuy graduates go on to Ivy League colleges,

in a city where less than half of students go on to college.[1] At least four alumni are Nobel laureates.

When I walked into the building on my first day, I heard a piano playing classical music. I wasn't sure where the sound was coming from, but I could tell I was hearing it distinctly from several rooms away. The acoustics were that good. By spending a few days wandering the hallways like a Brontë heroine in a country house, stunned and exhilarated, I discovered that the resources available to this academic elite included two lecture halls; a skylit cafeteria overlooking the Hudson River; swimming pools; labs for ceramics, photograph, wood, plastics, and robotics. During school hours, students were expected to conduct themselves like little adults, ready to get down to the business of being educated. After school, they participated in a symphony orchestra, elaborate theater productions, or a film appreciation club. The oddest thing I saw was the Museum room, which housed a replica of an old classroom—a memorial to the institution's scrappy origins: The Old Stuyvesant Campus in Gramercy was (in fitting with the meritocratic origin story) a notoriously dingy and uncomfortable old building and is as romanticized a place as any in New York City.

Founded in the early twentieth century with the intention of providing the most academically talented students with an exceptional education regardless of class background, selective-enrollment schools are the original American "choice"

---

1 "A Report from Research Alliance Explores NYC Students' Pathways into and through College," November 2014, steinhardt.nyu.edu.

schools—Eva Moskowitz, CEO of Success Academy Charter Schools, is a Stuyvesant alum.[2] Today, gifted and talented programs and magnet schools are still valued by urban planners and politicians for their ability to keep upper-middle-class people who would otherwise send their kids to private school or move to the suburbs in the city, and ensure their participation in the city's school system.[3] They are public schools, but like other "choice" schools with an admissions process, including charters, Specialized High Schools enroll far fewer children from low-income backgrounds, children with special needs, and English-language learners than traditional public schools.

The syllabus for the freshman composition course I taught at Stuyvesant included *Brave New World*, *Things Fall Apart*, *The Taming of the Shrew*, *Twelve Angry Men*, *1984*, *Julius Caesar*, a short fiction unit, and a poetry unit including poets ranging from Federico García Lorca to Nikki Giovanni, with an essay required in a different genre (argumentative, persuasive, etc.) for each text. Classroom conflicts took the form of intense verbal debates related to the text we happened to be reading at the time: the uproar from the female students when one boy argued, during a discussion about *The Taming of the Shrew*, that "women should listen to their husbands," for

---

2   The most well-received and successful of the major market-oriented choice reforms, charter schools are institutions—sometimes for-profit, sometimes not—that agree to meet an undefined higher standard of accountability in exchange for increased self-governance. Like gifted and talented programs, students must apply for entrance, but unlike those programs, they are aimed at providing general education.

3   Alia Wong, "The Cutthroat World of Elite Public Schools," *Atlantic*, December 4, 2014, theatlantic.com.

instance. Students acted out, but it was usually through passive aggression. Once, I found a Pepsi bottle full of urine placed precariously on a handrail over an immaculately clean stairwell. Another teacher told me she'd seen kids throw bottles of pee down the stairwells before as a form of quiet rebellion. The greatest challenge for a teacher was, as one colleague of mine put it, "pulling them out of their shells" during class.

Only a tiny fraction of American kids attend specialized public schools, and New York City stands alone in using a single standardized test as admissions criteria. Students admitted to any one of the Specialized High Schools in the city represent just 6 percent of its pool of eighth-graders applying for high schools.[4] The significance of these schools is not how many students they enroll. It's what they symbolize. Stuyvesant is free and consistently ranked among the top American high schools in *U.S. News & World Report*. It's something to aspire to. There are no dropouts, and the football team has a 91 percent grade average.[5] Strikingly for New York City, there are no metal detectors to pass through daily on your way to class. The only thing barring entry is invisible: the SHSAT exam.

As a beginning teacher, my job at Stuyvesant was first to observe, then become a coteacher of the class, then take over teaching the class myself.

---

4   Halley Potter and David Tipson, "Eliminate Gifted Tracks and Expand to a Schoolwide Approach," *New York Times*, June 4, 2014, nytimes.com.

5   Judie Glave, "New York's Stuyvesant High School, A Young Achiever's Dream," *Los Angeles Times*, December 30, 1990, latimes.com.

My cooperating teacher, the experienced teacher who would guide me through the process, believed in a "sink or swim" mentality and gave me three days to observe, a week and a half to coteach, and the rest of the semester on my own. He warned me about the pressure put on his students by parents and faculty. In my observation notes from the time, I wrote earnestly: "He tries to assign only 45 minutes of homework each day, because when he asks his kids how many hours of sleep they got the previous night, many of them answer 'five.' Too many of them are depressed because they are overworked" from homework in other classes. One boy of fifteen showed up every day that first week of the semester without saying a word during our forty-minute period, except "Here" when his name was called during attendance. The next week, he was not there. The cooperating teacher shrugged and told me that he'd had a nervous breakdown and refused to do anything but sit at home and play video games. He did not return. In fact, it's not abnormal for a few students a semester to take weeks or months off from school because of stress. In "Confronting Mental Health Issues at Stuyvesant," health journalist Rong Xiaoqing reports that the deputy director of a nonprofit community organization in the Lower East Side, Hamilton-Madison House, told her he sees more students from Stuy than any other school.[6]

Throughout the semester we taught together, the cooperating teacher I worked with encouraged me to ensure that

6   Rong Xiaoqing, "Confronting Mental Health Issues at Stuyvesant," *Voices of NY*, January 21, 2014, voicesofny.org.

every single voice in the classroom was heard. His own method of doing so was to scream "Louder!" or "Speak up!" over a student who spoke too quietly. This went against everything I'd been taught in the school of education where I was taking classes at night—and which, like many schools of education, emphasized student-centered, progressive pedagogy—but the teacher also worked hard to create an environment of mutual respect and trust, especially through humor, and was popular among many students and had been teaching at the school since the 1970s. He was referred to affectionately as "old school" by other faculty. I saw him use this approach equally to boys and girls; at the end of one class, a male student said, "That's why I love this class!" and tried to hug his teacher.

Participation was high—we kept a record on a yellow legal pad, putting a check next to the student's name whenever a hand was raised—but three kids out of our thirty-one students never volunteered and, when called upon, looked as if they were in pain. At one point during the first few weeks of class, one of the girls mentioned to me after class that she felt afraid to volunteer. Attributing this reluctance to a student's personality as some teachers do ("She's just shy!") is inadequate, since like all human beings, children act like "different people" in different circumstances, adapting and responding based on their background and perceptions. When I asked the cooperating teacher what we could do to try to involve the students who never participated in discussion or homework assignments, he responded, "They'll probably fail this semester." It wasn't a glib response; it came

from experience, for this was the way the school was structured, and though the teacher repeatedly expressed concern
with the organizational philosophy of the school, it was
ingrained in school culture and policies. Instruction was for
the gifted and talented, the thinking went, and took place at a
rapid pace—if you couldn't keep up, what were you doing
there?

After my teaching day ended, I spent time tutoring students
individually and in groups at the Writing Center in the
library. During one-on-one sessions of about twenty to thirty
minutes each, students (some of whom were "regulars,"
signing up to attend once a week, others stopping by with
looks of desperation on their faces the day before a major
paper was due) were surprised to find support. At the Writing
Center, I worked with a tenth-grader on a literary essay about
how the competitive values of American society influenced
Fitzgerald's *Great Gatsby*; the student connected the wealth
disparities and competition of 1920s America to the school
environment, writing that the obsession with grades and
getting into an Ivy League college had impeded his ability to
make meaningful relationships with his peers.

In an article published in the school newspaper in 2010, a
graduating senior wrote about the way his perspective on the
school culture evolved from his first day to his last:
"Community is not a word to describe [our school].
Competition is a better synonym." The anxieties of students,
parents, teachers, and administration about college entrance
and future performance was a vicious cycle assuring that the
school environment would be a competitive pressure cooker.

He noted that nothing had really changed since the principal had addressed students' concerns about communication and the problem of competition in 1984. To get a "good" education, he wrote, students needed to be able to see the school in a different light, "not as a brewing hot pot for college, but as a place where . . . teachers, parents, and students, can learn from and with each other."[7]

In the same issue, a student defended his choice to drop out of the school as a response to the school's policy for dealing with "delinquents": "The first weapon is punishment," writes Wes Schierenbeck, and the next is isolation.[8] He wrote about how caring for a disabled parent led him to seek confidence and encouragement from after-school programs, from which he was paradoxically removed as his grades began to slip. When he explained his situation to an assistant principal—"I remember once telling her, near tears over being pulled from a show, that what I really cared about was theater, and that academics was second priority for me." Her response, according to the student: "You should've gone to LaGuardia."

The fact is, the school is explicitly *not* for everyone. It's an example of the best the traditional model of education has to offer. For the most part, students succeed based on the metrics typically used to evaluate high schools: how many students gain acceptance to a prestigious college. An English teacher at the school told me, "Competition and community are not

7   Alexander Huang, "The House Will Not Hold: Diary of a Mad Senior," *The Spectator*, June 4, 2010, p. 14.
8   Wes Schierenbeck, "Stuyvesant's Policy on Delinquency: Who's Dumb Now?" *The Spectator*, June 4, 2010, p. 14.

two mutually exclusive things. Just because we have one doesn't mean we can't have the other." But the assumptions that underlie this arrangement are the same ones that underlie our entire system of education: that "high-achieving" individuals benefit most from seclusion from the rest of us; that what benefits high-achieving individuals is more important than what benefits the community as a whole; that a student's understanding is best evaluated based on her individual performance and best expressed on a one-hundred-point scale; that individual performance is more important than empathy, or an aptitude for explaining concepts to peers.

It's easy to see how this translates into the world of work: A student raised to be competitive on standardized tests might be prepared both academically and emotionally for a job in the tech or finance industries, while a student with developed socio-emotional skills would fit seamlessly into a service-sector job like teaching or nursing.

Specialized schools are seen as "tiny islands of achievement in a vast sea of mediocrity."[9] In *City Journal*, the magazine that was also a self-proclaimed idea factory for the "reviving" of New York City under the conservative Giuliani administration, conservative writer Heather MacDonald rails against the schools' critics, who argue that high-performing students should not be "skimmed" from their local schools to citywide gifted and talented programs:

---

9   Heather MacDonald, "How Gotham's Elite High Schools Escaped the Leveller's Ax," *City Journal*, January 1, 1999, city-journal.org.

Every school needs academically excited children to moti-
vate the others, the argument goes, so the smartest
shouldn't be skimmed off and put in separate schools. But
surely it is the teacher's responsibility, not the students', to
inspire the laggards. If an academically motivated student
would reach his fullest potential in an environment of his
peers, it is educational exploitation to deny him that environment in the hope that he will kindle the interest of
academically uninspired students.

Who are "the laggards"? Who are "the gifted"?
MacDonald's argument seems to suggest that personality,
motivation, and intelligence are fixed entities intrinsic to
individuals—that a student walks into the classroom and
leaves it the same exact person. But personality and motivation change depending on the context, and even IQ—which
is far from a perfect proxy for intelligence, but which is at
least quantifiable—changes over the course of an individual's
life span and over generations.[10] (In the past hundred years,
the IQ of the general population in the United States has
risen, which researchers attribute to increased and widespread access to schooling.[11]) When I hear a teacher refer to a
student as a "shy kid," I ask them if they have seen that

10   Scott Barry Kaufman, "Intelligence Is Still Not Fixed at Birth,"
Psychology Today, October 21, 2011, psychologytoday.com; and Elizabeth
Sowell et al., "Mapping Cortical Change across the Human Life Span,"
Nature Neuroscience 6 (2003): 309–15, nature.com.
11   Clancy Blair et al., "Rising Mean IQ: Cognitive Demand of
Mathematics Education for Young Children, Population Exposure to Formal
Schooling, and the Neurobiology of the Prefrontal Cortex," *Intelligence* 33,
no. 1 (January–February 2005): 93–106, sciencedirect.com.

student in another class, or at home, or hanging out with friends. As a one-time "shy kid," I know that my mother and sisters and best friends would never have described me that way. But my math teacher would have, because I despised him with every fiber of my teenage being and considered myself incapable of learning algebra, especially from him.

In MacDonald's accounting of the teacher-student relationship, teachers sound a lot like managers in the workplace—accountable for sparking passion and understanding in her students, or direct reports. But being inspired by peers is not exploitation; it's collaboration.

And if access to "gifted" education could be made equitable—a theoretical question at this point—why must gifted students be segregated from others to fulfill their own potential? Federal law requires that students with special education needs be educated in the least restrictive environment possible, which frequently translates, or should, to inclusion with general education students. On the other hand, the implication of separate "gifted and talented" programs is that genius must be cloistered into elite, competitive enclaves, and that a fundamental task of schooling is to select and nurture the most inspired students with the best resources available.

This is particularly troubling when we consider the demographic breakdown of these separate gifted programs. Stuyvesant's student demographics are dramatically different from New York City's: 69 percent Asian or Native Hawaiian/Pacific Islander; 25 percent white; 3 percent Latino; and 2 percent Black. As a whole, the school enrolls lower-than-average numbers of students whose household income qualifies them for free or reduced-price lunch (49 percent of New York state and 72 percent of NYC public school students overall, compared to Stuy's 37 percent).

Most New York City public schools do not have swimming pools or robotics labs. Some are not even fit for daily use. A building assessment survey of Catherine and Count Basie Middle School in Jamaica, Queens—where Black students make up 72 percent of the student body, and 82 percent of students are eligible for free lunch[12]—noted that, "After the removal of the burned-out ballasts in the Principal's office, the room still cannot be used due to a severe odor." At the time the building was surveyed, in 2011, there were also inoperative light fixtures and a roof repair project causing leaks into classrooms and the gym. In 2013, the Service Employees International Union (SEIU) released a research report on New York City's public schools showing that as the percentage of students who qualify for free or reduced-price lunch at a city school increases, the school's score on building maintenance and cleanliness decreases. Students from the poorest families attend school in the most neglected buildings, according to the report.[13] The SEIU also noted that polychlorinated biphenyls, a toxic compound found in light fixtures that hinders cognitive development, causes cancer, and was banned by Congress in the 1970s, are present in New York City schools. Schools on the waitlist to have their toxic

12   Insideschools review of M.S. 72 Catherine and Count Basie, insideschools.org.
13   SEIU Local 32BJ, "Falling Further Apart: Decaying Schools in New York City's Poorest Neighborhoods," seiu32bj.org.

light fixtures replaced tended to have a higher percentage of
nonwhite students and students receiving free lunch than
schools where the fixtures had already been replaced.[14]

A parent at Dos Puentes, in Washington Heights, told *New
York* magazine that kids came home from school covered in
urine. The stall doors frequently do not open, and kids have
to crawl out from under them on the floor.[15] In 2013, a group
of parents at Public School 58 in Carroll Gardens made a
video of their school's bathrooms, with broken toilet seats,
burned-out light fixtures, and rusted air vents. They won
$110,000 in a competition for city funding.[16]

One hundred thousand New York City school students
pass through permanent metal detectors to get to school each
day.[17] During the 2004–05 school year, 82 percent of children
who attended high schools with permanent metal detectors in
place were Black or Latino, and 60 percent were from low-
income families.[18] Armed police officers are also part of the
routine in some schools.

One year after I finished student teaching at Stuyvesant,
the NAACP Legal Defense Fund (LDF) filed a federal civil

---

14   Ibid.
15   Caroline Bankoff, "Washington Heights School's Bathrooms Are So
Broken That Kids Are Coming Home Covered in Pee," *New York*, December
10, 2014, nymag.com.
16   Mark Morales, "Video of Smelly Carroll Gardens Public School
Bathrooms Wins Contest for City Funds," *Daily News*, April 10, 2013, nyda-
ilynews.com.
17   NYCLU, "A Look at New York City School Safety," nyclu.org/files/
a_look_at_new_york_city_school_safety.pdf;   nesri.org/sites/default/files/
NYC_FactSheet_Discipline_Policing.pdf.
18   New York Civil Liberties Union, "School to Prison Pipeline: A
Look at School Safety," nyclu.org.

rights complaint against the NYC Department of Education and its Specialized High Schools, pointing out that gifted and talented public schools are among the most segregated in the city, and that the disparities are connected at least in part to admissions policies that rely on standardized tests. Indeed, in 2014, 70 percent of New York City's eighth-graders were Black or Latino, but only 11 percent of students admitted to Specialized High Schools were. Thirty percent of students are female and 70 percent are male.

Along with the LDF, the American Psychological Association, the American Educational Research Association, and the National Council on Measurement in Education all say that high-stakes decisions with implications on access to education should never be made on the basis of results from one exam.

There is no doubt that the stakes of the Specialized High School exam are high. The independent nonprofit news organization ProPublica analyzed federal education data representing more than three-quarters of American public school children to examine whether children in high-poverty schools have the same access to advanced courses and content and special programs as children in other schools. Nationwide, the answer was a clear and resounding no.[19]

There is also no doubt that even if the test is fair, the game is rigged. The authors of a study that closely examined the

---

19 Jennifer LaFleur, Al Shaw, Sharona Coutts, and Jeff Larson, "The Opportunity Gap: Is Your State Providing Equal Access to Education?" ProPublica, updated January 24, 2013, projects.propublica.org; and Stuyvesant High School report, projects.propublica.org.

entire process of entry to New York City's Specialized High Schools, from application, admission, and matriculation, were able to trace a "pipeline" of students flowing from a small number of (highly selective) middle schools to specialized high schools.[20] Girls, Latinos, and low-income students were all found to be less likely to take the admissions test than prior academic achievement would predict. Both of these findings suggest that the outcome of who attends these schools and who does not is influenced by social and economic factors, not just individual intelligence or drive.

Yet administrators continue to cling to the illusion that the exams are impartial, identifying the most gifted students of all backgrounds, for the same reason that kids will always love *Harry Potter* and *Cinderella*. The idea that you—or your child—has a secret, hidden specialness inside waiting to come out and swing the doors of opportunity wide open, is a deeply appealing one. Getting an offer to go to Stuyvesant is like winning a golden ticket: rare, exhilarating, a way out of mediocrity and deficiency and on to excellence and wealth. Stanley Teitel, principal of Stuyvesant until a cheating scandal in 2014 finally ended his career, expressed his disdain for the view that the schools consider more than just the outcome of a single standardized test in the admissions process back in 1971, when he was chairman of the physics department: "I don't care if your mommy or daddy knows the

---

20   Sean P. Corcoran and Christine Baker-Smith, "Pathways to an Elite Education: Application, Admission, and Matriculation to New York City's Specialized High Schools," *Research Alliance for New York City Schools*, 2015, steinhardt.nyu.edu.

superintendent of the borough ... I don't want to know anything else—no portfolios, not any of the other crap!"[21] His emotional response to the mere suggestion of using a broader assessment strategy for admissions—palpable disgust—shows the investment that many have in the idea of having been impartially selected to attend. Many Stuy parents buy T-shirts with the name of the high school printed on the front and actually wear them.

Portfolios may be "crap" your mommy and daddy can help you assemble, but standardized performance tests also fail as a metric for assessing human potential. Since the goal of meritocrats is to locate, nurture, and reward those who truly excel, they are always searching for the most objective methods of comparison. But it doesn't matter how many times they are modified: The tests will continue to be biased, both on their own terms and because they are the products of a deeply unequal society. The overwhelming evidence that culturally, linguistically, and ethnically diverse students and poor students (and, in gifted and talented science and math classes, female students) are underrepresented in gifted and talented programs nationwide—while being overrepresented in special education programs—suggests that the formal and informal selection process for the programs is anything but neutral. Large-scale group differences in test outcomes have been observed routinely since the beginning of modern psychological testing. Gaps between Black people and white

---

21   Heather MacDonald, "How Gotham's Elite High Schools Escaped the Leveller's Ax," *City Journal*, January 1, 1999, city-journal.org.

people, rich people and poor people, and men and women, have been explained as the product of genetics (a conservative viewpoint best represented by the field of eugenics, and its modern incarnation, Charles Murray and Richard Herrnstein's 1994 book *The Bell Curve*), as the product of an impoverished upbringing (the liberal perspective behind the compensatory education efforts of the Johnson administration in the 1960s), or as the fault of the tests.[22] In 2010, the Supreme Court ruled in favor of a group of 6,000 Black firefighters who claimed the city's use of a written application test had unfairly barred them from being hired.[23] In 2012, a federal judge ruled that a New York State teaching certification test that Blacks and Latinos passed at lower rates than whites was discriminatory, and ordered the city to pay years of back wages to thousands of teachers who'd been demoted or denied a job on the basis of the results. Two years later, the city rolled out new, more difficult tests, and another discrimination case was filed, which was under consideration as of April 2015.[24]

---

22   Claude Steele, a psychologist at Teachers College, has found that when women were told before a math test, "This is a test where women always do as well as men," they performed just as well as men; when they were not, they scored, on average, a whole standard deviation below men. Likewise, when a group of Black students was given a standard IQ test and told it was a puzzle that has nothing to do with abilities, they performed exactly the same as white students, but Black students who knew they were taking an IQ test performed a full standard deviation worse than white students. Steele has written about what he calls "stereotype threat" in *Whistling Vivaldi: How Stereotypes Affect Us and What We Can Do* (New York: W. W. Norton, 2011).

23   Robert Barnes, "Justices Say Employers May Not Use Discriminatory Testing Practices," *Washington Post*, May 25, 2010, washingtonpost.com.

24   Kate Taylor, "Questions of Bias Are Raised about a Teachers' Exam

This presents a real intellectual problem for earnest meritocrats unconvinced by the sham science of eugenics. Some resolve the cognitive dissonance by flattening the problem altogether, focusing on how to "identify gifted minorities," rather than challenge the foundational proposition of giftedness. In "Gifted, Talented, and Underserved," Chester E. Finn Jr., senior fellow at the Hoover Institution, laments that

> many of the country's most talented young people—rich and poor alike—are left unable to surge ahead, languishing in classes geared toward universal but modest proficiency. In our effort to leave no child behind, we are failing the high-ability children who are the most likely to become tomorrow's scientists, inventors, poets, and entrepreneurs—and in the process we risk leaving our nation behind.

The failure, he insists, is due more to political correctness than it is to scarce resources.[25] Finn holds up the Knowledge Is Power Program (KIPP) network—the largest charter chain in the country, known for popularizing "no excuses" discipline—as a model for schools that can "change the trajectory of the lives of gifted, poor children" (provided, he notes, that "families are willing to enroll them, get them to school regularly, and tolerate a demanding academic schedule"). Founded in 1994, KIPP schools have been awarded

in New York," *New York Times*, April 7, 2015, nytimes.com.
25   Chester E. Finn Jr., "Gifted, Talented, and Underserved," *National Affairs* 18 (Winter 2014), nationalaffairs.com.

hundreds of millions of dollars in grants from philanthrocapitalists including the Gates Foundation and the Walton
Family Foundation,[26] but their methods for motivating
students are severe: Desks are taken away from students as a
form of punishment. Kids routinely receive suspensions for
dress code infractions[27] and refer to the schools as the Kids in
Prison Program.[28] "It's like treating [students] like animals,"
one former KIPP teacher told AlterNet.[29] Upper-middle-
class parents would riot before allowing their own children to
be subjected to an education that is more like a baptism by fire
than a learning experience. Low-income families, on the
other hand, don't always have the same social power and
connections to call on, and sometimes embrace the promise
of such tactics to correct antisocial behavior, accurately
perceiving the deeply lower margin of error allowed for a
poor kid versus a rich one in American society.

Other defenders of gifted programs, like the executive
director of the New York Campaign for Achievement Now
(who's a board member for the Success Academy charter
network), acknowledge the schools' lack of diversity and
express concern but ultimately come down in favor of

---

26   "KIPP Receives $7.9 Million to Enter World of High School," Bill
and Melinda Gates Foundation, gatesfoundation.org; and "$25 Million
Investment in KIPP to Help Double Number of Families That Choose
KIPP Schools," Walton Family Foundation, November 15, 2011, waltonfa-
milyfoundation.org.

27   James Horn, "KIPP Forces 5th Graders to 'Earn' Desks by Sitting
on the Floor for a Week," AlterNet, December 17, 2013, alternet.org.

28   Sarah Carr, "The Painful Backlash against 'No-Excuses' School
Discipline," *Hechinger Report*, November 17, 2014, hechingerreport.org.

29   Horn, "KIPP Forces 5th Graders to 'Earn' Desks."

admissions based only on performance: "Diversity is a laudable goal in public education and one that I support, but excellence is more important still—regardless of the optics of student diversity."[30]

While the citywide programs are the most prestigious in New York City, disparities exist among districts and even in schools where gifted classes take place alongside general education classes. The "optics" are particularly striking in New York City. For example, in District 3, which covers the Upper West Side, there are five gifted and talented programs. District 7, which covers the South Bronx—one of the poorest districts in the country, as well as one with a marked majority of Black and Latino residents—has none.[31] In most schools that house both gifted and general education programs, gifted classes are filled with white students, while general education classes are comprised almost entirely of Black and Latino students.

Inequalities have been exacerbated in New York City by Bloomberg-era testing reforms. While districts were once able to create gifted and talented classes on an as-needed basis using their own methods of evaluation, the Bloomberg administration eliminated teacher evaluations and classroom observation as methods for determining the need for such programs and required the use of two high-stakes tests administered

---

30   Derrell Bradford, "In Defense of the City's Selective High Schools," CUNY Institute for Education Policy, January 26, 2015, ciep.hunter.cuny.edu.

31   Al Baker, "Gifted, Talented and Separated: In One School, Students Are Divided by Gifted Label—And Race," *New York Times*, January 12, 2013, nytimes.com.

back-to-back to assess students. Intended to increase fairness, the change actually decreased diversity, as Al Baker reported in the *New York Times*, "with children from the poorest districts offered a smaller share of kindergarten gifted slots" and kids in wealthier districts getting more.[32]

"It's not our fault," responded one parent, who chose to remain anonymous. "We want the best for our children."

That parent is right. Studies have shown that when selecting schools, parents of all backgrounds are highly attentive to demographics—that is, they seek out schools in which their child will not be a minority—while at the same time expressing idealistic preference for integrated public schools.

This is a systematic problem with parental choice. Individual priorities hardly ever reflect collective priorities. Privately, parents will almost always act in what they see as the best interest of their child, even if that interest conflicts with their values and has the unintended consequence of furthering social inequities—and it is hard to fault them, since this is their role, as it is now both culturally and legally understood. Which is why, in a democracy, policy-making should not be a matter of individual choice, but a macro-level plan that reflects the values of people acting in coordination. In a society organized around private and unregulated ownership of industry and trade—free-market capitalism— our individual choices do not express our priorities; they express what we think we need to do to survive. There is a fundamental difference.

---

32   Ibid.

At Stuyvesant, one of the books I taught, *Truancy* by Isamu Fukui, was written by a former student and is dedicated "to anyone who has ever suffered in the name of education." In it, bands of dropouts calling themselves Truants struggle to take down their city's government, ruled by an autocratic mayor who directs a police force of Educators. The kids loved it. It spoke to the common and visceral ways in which school can be a fundamentally nightmarish experience for kids, but also to the more specific dystopia of capitalist schooling—where school systems are de facto sorting grounds locking people into their fated class position with each step (à la Ayn Rand's *Atlas Shrugged*, and *Brave New World*), and students often engaged self-consciously in a fight over limited resources—open college seats, future jobs. It is literally a fight to the death, like in *The Hunger Games* (another student favorite, as I would later find)—or at least, a fight over who will get a job that offers health care, vacation days, retirement, maybe even meaningful work, and who will get a job that pays minimum wage with no benefits, or remain persistently unemployed. And in high school, as in dystopian fiction, the struggle extends beyond the individual to the collective. Individual values and dreams are in clear conflict with societal demands. The Truants want freedom in a punishing, conformist world. Huxley's John "the Savage" desires passion and art in a society that values stability. Kids want to be respected, creative, powerful, and to have friends—but the free-market capitalist economy requires only managers—practical and ruthlessly ambitious—or employees who can provide service with a smile.

I've taught *Brave New World* twice, once to kids at Stuy
and another time to kids at a school with a student body
comprised mostly of low-income students, and been
shocked both times at the brilliant, almost preternatural
analysis that dystopian novels bring out in so many students,
despite the difficulty of the language. In fact, several of the
tenth-graders I taught at the Young Women's Leadership
School[33] hated *Brave New World*, not because it was bleak or
sad, but because it was obvious. Teens haven't yet quite
been stamped by society as "undeserving" or not, but they
are about to be, and they know it. Every few years they are
subjected to an admissions contest with inexplicable, rigged
results.

More than half a century after *Brown v. Board of Education*,
which ruled that segregated schools are unconstitutional, our
nation's schools are more segregated than ever by race, class,
and ability, despite decades of research documenting the
long-term harm it does to children from low-income families. Ability grouping, which was originally promoted as a
way for teachers and schools to teach to the needs of different
learners, instead segregates students based on low socioeconomic status and race into separate tracks that translate, often
explicitly, to life paths. In elementary school, gifted, average,
and below-average groups might be labeled "Red," "Yellow,"
and "Blue" or given cute animal names like "Lions" and

33   At Young Women's Leadership School, a higher number of students
than the state or district average receive free or reduced-price lunch. The
number of students receiving free or reduced-price lunch is a rough indicator of socioeconomic class status in education policy. Young Women's
Leadership School report, projects.propublica.org.

"Tigers," but by high school, the distinction is clear: "College Prep" or "Vocational."[34] Positive effects on students in the "high ability" groupings have been shown to be negligible, while negative effects are deleterious—which should be unsurprising in the context of an economy where the definitions of "excellence" and "competence" are collapsed.[35] Further, the "track" metaphor is a compelling mirror of the highly stratified American economy, with wealthy CEOs at the very top, the upper middle class struggling to stay there, and everyone else in a race to the bottom.

Homework also serves to further social stratification in schools. The number of hours of homework assigned has been given enormous emphasis—particularly in charter schools—since the landmark 1980s report *A Nation at Risk* recommended that high school students be given more homework to increase the quality and international competitiveness of American education in the 1980s. Prior to that, in the 1950s, researchers had found that "compulsory homework does not result in sufficiently improved academic accomplishments to justify retention."[36] In 1968, researchers argued that it is actively harmful to students, writing that "whenever homework crowds out social experience, outdoor recreation, and creative activities, and whenever it usurps time devoted

34 "Research Spotlight on Academic Ability Grouping," National Education Association, nea.org.
35 William Mathis, "Moving beyond Tracking," *Research-Based Options for Education Policymaking* (University of Colorado Boulder: National Education Policy Center, 2013), nepc.colorado.edu.
36 H. J. Otto, "Elementary Education—III. Organization and Administration," in W. S. Monroe, ed., *Encyclopedia of Educational Research* (New York: Macmillan, 1950), 380.

to sleep, it is not meeting the basic needs of children and adolescents."[37]

A more recent research review of studies conducted from 1989–2003 found that there was little to no difference in achievement among elementary schoolers who were assigned homework versus those who were assigned none at all.[38] No research has ever shown that homework benefits young children, even on standardized test performance. But it does increase a student's working day to eight or sometimes even ten or eleven hours. Today it continues to be assigned today throughout K–12 education, and as early as *preschool*.[39]

It is a double shift for middle-class children and a *triple shift* for children in low-income families who work after-school jobs or take care of siblings, which corresponds to the second shifts taken on by working mothers.

So why is homework still part of the educational system? Perhaps it is because most of today's teachers and parents grew up on it themselves. Or perhaps it's because both teachers and parents are afraid of what will happen if they do not

37   Statement from the American Educational Research Association (in P. R. Wildman, "Homework Pressures," *Peabody Journal of Education*, 204) accessed in 1968, Cathy Vatterott, *Rethinking Homework: Best Practices That Support Diverse Needs* (Alexandria, VA: Association for Supervision and Curriculum Development, 2009), 6.

38   Harris Cooper, "Does Homework Improve Academic Achievement? If So, How Much Is Best?" *SEDL Letter* 20, no. 2 (August 2008), sedl.org.

39   See Sara Bennett and Nancy Kalish, *The Case against Homework: How Homework Is Hurting Our Children and What We Can Do about It* (New York: Crown, 2006); Alfie Kohn, *The Homework Myth: Why Our Kids Get Too Much of a Bad Thing* (Cambridge, MA: Da Capo Press, 2006); Etta Kralovec and John Buell, *The End of Homework: How Homework Disrupts Families, Overburdens Children, and Limits Learning* (Boston: Beacon Press, 2000).

require it. The ritual of leaving school only to start homework accustoms children to the rhythm of the never-ending American workday. It teaches children to think about learning in terms of productivity—math problems completed, hours spent—and to manage their time accordingly.

And it's yet another way that the wealthy can afford to give their children a competitive edge. "We should be asking if the real reason we're not saying no to preschool homework is because, in today's rush to get young children into academics, we fear our child will fall behind," wrote one parent in a *New York Times* op-ed.[40] A piece in the *Atlantic* is titled, "My Daughter's Homework Is Killing Me."[41] Nagging has become part of the job of parenting for middle-class parents, and graded homework assignments reward children and families whose parents are there hanging over their shoulders, perfecting their science projects or even just available to answer questions.

Just as unfair advantages are handed out to children on the basis of class, so discipline is meted out to children on the basis of race. In the past twenty-five years, schools' adoption of "zero tolerance" policies has led to an overall dramatic increase in suspensions and expulsions—even though subjection to disciplinary actions has been linked to lower graduation rates and increased rates of criminal activity later in life. A 2014 Department of Education analysis of data from the

40 Holly Korbey, "Should Preschoolers Have Homework?" *Motherlode* (blog), *New York Times*, February 22, 2012, parenting.blogs.nytimes.com.
41 Karl Taro Greenfeld, "My Daughter's Homework Is Killing Me," *Atlantic*, October 2013, theatlantic.com.

past fifteen years has shown that Black children are more likely than white children to face severe punishments for perceived misbehaviors and are suspended and expelled at three times the rate of white students. This includes girls as well as boys: During the 2012 school year, Black girls in public schools were suspended at a rate of 12 percent, in comparison to 2 percent for white girls. The disparities in enforcement of discipline begin in preschool—close to half of all children who are expelled from preschool are Black. This is due at least in part to the fact that Black children are frequently viewed as older and less innocent than white children.[42]

I asked Michael G. Wilson, professor of inclusive education and director of Teachers College's School to Prison Pipeline Project, which researches the education and incarceration of youth about these disparities (Teachers College is one of the top graduate schools of education in the country). Wilson told me,

> It clearly goes back to the entire formation of the idea of how we view schooling in this country. Immediately, certain kids belong in certain places. Then we create the systems to figure out who these kids are. We base it off of the tradition of what it means to be "normal"

—what "normal" looks like and acts like and what families it comes from.

Wilson began his career teaching students labeled with

---

42   "Black Boys Viewed as Older, Less Innocent Than Whites, Research Finds," American Psychological Association, March 6, 2014, apa.org.

emotional disorders and left after three years, when he realized that his own strong belief in educating the whole person, which he believes interests kids in learning, was at odds with the school system he taught in. He said:

> I was more focused on getting them to think about the information they were reading in government class—why does it matter for them today, how can they use it in the future to their advantage, what are the problems in their own lives? I would stop class to discuss problems in kids' lives. And that's what matters to me, which didn't really fit with what was going on in the schools.

As the War on Drugs of the 1980s became a War on Adolescents, students were treated increasingly as either victims or suspects. An atmosphere of surveillance of teachers and students pervades schools serving people of all backgrounds and classes, except the very wealthy. According to the National Center for Education Statistics, higher percentages of public than of private schools report the use of metal detectors and security cameras, random dog sniffs to search for drugs, the requirement that backpacks be clear plastic or not brought to school at all, and random sweeps for contraband. Sixty-four percent of American public schools use video cameras to monitor the halls, and 24 percent use dogs to search for drugs. Each of these actions is categorized under school safety and security measures.[43]

---

43   "Fast Facts: School Safety and Security Measures," National Center for Education Statistics, nces.ed.gov.

Worse, the system incentivizes teachers to expel kids who are "behavioral problems" or "low performers" from the classroom. "It seems like education policy people are often of this mindset that impacts of education policy are always good," says Wilson. "This movement towards accountability, merit pay, and so forth has been and will continue to be this sort of drive to keep the best students and find any way that you can to remove the 'worst' students."

It gives us incentives to label students as "smart kids," "good kids," or "bad kids," he explained. "There has to be some sort of addressing of that and this policy, and the issues of accountability, and what that sets up in school," he said. Wilson is working with colleagues to find ways to communicate to teachers the impact of discipline codes that require the removal of a student from a classroom, and to formulate alternatives.

In an era of high expectations, administrators and policymakers demand from teachers the illusion of control over students. New York City teacher William Johnson wrote a notorious op-ed for the *New York Times* called "Confessions of a 'Bad' Teacher,"[44] describing the contradictory and unsupported guidance he received from evaluations in the public school system. Johnson spent several years as a New York City public school teacher before being denied tenure and leaving to take a job at the prestigious Upper East Side private school Spence. In the public school system, a

---

44 William Johnson, "Confessions of a 'Bad' Teacher," *New York Times*, March 3, 2012, nytimes.com.

teacher's worst nightmare is, he explained to me in an interview in the fall of 2014, "if the assistant principal walks in and the lesson is not working, you're freaked out. It's terrifying." At Spence, he is not afraid to try new things or experiment, because failure does not mean losing his job or being labeled "unsatisfactory."

Schools do not exist in a vacuum. For all our focus on what goes on inside them, it is housing policy more than anything that determines educational access and perpetuates educational inequality.[45]

In the United States, the federal government provides only about 10 to 15 percent of funding for public schools, while local districts and states provide the rest, usually from property taxes. This is in stark contrast to other industrial countries, which provide about half of funding through centralized sources. In the United States, education is the biggest item in state and local budgets, and the largest portion of each property owner's property taxes goes to their local public schools.

Children's schooling is tied to their parents' private property or neighborhood through this uniquely decentralized system of funding schools. Income differences between neighborhoods and districts are thus replicated in public schools, with the poorest schools in the poorest neighborhoods receiving the least amount of funding and resources,

---

45   Jane Gingrich and Ben Ansell, "Sorting for Schools: Housing, Education and Inequality," *Socio-Economic Review* 12, no. 2 (2014): 329–51, ser.oxfordjournals.org.

and schools in wealthy neighborhoods receiving the most.

For example, in 1999, the *Charlotte Observer* documented that "in each of the Carolinas, the fifteen poorest school systems post test scores that repeatedly pull both states down on national education measures, such as the SAT." Mecklenburg, one of the most affluent districts in North Carolina, spent an estimated $5,529 per student that school year. The state's poorest district, Hoke County, spent only $708 per student.[46] Nearly a decade later, a staff reporter at the *Chicago Tribune* confirmed the trend, finding that 80 percent of school districts with large numbers of low-income students spent less per pupil than the state average.[47] In 2013, the *New York Times* reported that property taxes in the poorest 10 percent of school districts in New York resulted in $287,000 of funds per student, versus $1.9 million in the state's richest districts.[48]

Test scores from the wealthiest districts in the United States (which have the highest levels of funding and serve the lowest number of impoverished students) are comparable to those of countries like Japan and Hong Kong at the top of international test score comparisons. In contrast, the two worst-scoring US entities as of 2002 were the Miami-Dade County Public Schools in Florida and the Rochester City School District in New York. Both receive low levels of

---

46   Debbie Cenziper and Ted Mellnik, "The Price of Hope: Investigating Disparities among Rich and Poor Schools," *Nieman Reports*, March 15, 1999, niemanreports.org.

47   Diane Rado, "Rich School, Poor School," *Chicago Tribune*, February 4, 2007, chicagotribune.com.

48   Eduardo Porter, "In Public Education, Edge Still Goes to Rich," *New York Times*, November 5, 2013, nytimes.com.

funding and serve many poor students, and rank similarly to the lowest nations in international test score comparisons—Turkey, Jordan, and Iran.[49]

The American school system fails both in its execution and its ethos to give all children equal access to a good education. School alone can never serve as the great equalizer of society by giving kids the opportunity to raise their social standing in life. But it is still critical that American schools be radically transformed. The quality of education public school children experience is important not just because children's futures matter—but because their present matters.

Beyond the dystopia, there's a latent idea of a classless society in public schools: They are, in meritocratic and democratic society, theoretically a space and a system where *all* American children spend their days together, engaged in the collective project of socialization and learning. It's the ideal of public education as part of a social "commons" that makes the schools such an important target for conservatives as well as neoliberal privatizers. "So long as government owns and operates 90 percent of the schools in the United States, we have no right to expect that fewer than 90 percent of students who graduate are socialists," said Joseph Bast, CEO of the Heartland Institute.

For liberals, "the commons" of public education gives the illusion of a level playing field where individual merit can be proven. But the classlessness of public education will remain

---

49   Bruce J. Biddle and David C. Berliner, "A Research Synthesis: Unequal School Funding in the United States," *Educational Leadership* 59, no. 8 (May 2002): 48–59, ascd.org.

an illusion as long as it's a sphere within a wildly unequal and class-stratified nation (and world). As social inequalities worsen, is it any wonder that the liberal education reform project can grows more feverish and more punishing?

Should public schooling be a state project?

Schools play an essential—but, as we have seen, not the *only*—role in maintaining and deepening existing social and economic inequities.

That's why, like many student teachers, I'd been offended by the idea of myself as an authority figure. Standing in front of the class at the chalkboard felt like a lie. Was I smarter than my students? No. Did I know more about the subject I was teaching? Not always. I was so afraid of humiliating kids that I refused to call on a student unless her hand was raised.

In practice, that meant that over and over again I gave a lot of outgoing kids the chance to speak while effectively ignoring the ones who weren't interested. When no one's hand was raised, I wasted time wondering what to do next. In the middle of the semester, my students filled out their evaluations. "Dear Ms. Erickson," one student wrote, "when no one raises their hand, it's okay to *just call on someone*." He was right. It was OK. I'd been protecting tenth-graders from something they were perfectly prepared to face.

It is this false and misguided sense of children's fragile identity that informs the educational philosophy of "unschooling," an educational philosophy that is often championed as an alternative to the mainstream conception of education, in which children's education is self-guided, consisting of anything from books to episodes of *The Simpsons*, with no curriculum, assignments, or assessments. Demographically, unschooling is homeschooling for middle-class people with master's degrees, as it is for homeschooling in general: For example, in a 1998 volunteer survey of home-schooling families, only 0.8 percent had an income less than $10,000 in comparison to 12.6 percent for families with children nationally; 94 percent of the survey participants were white. Five years later, random-sample surveys conducted by the National Center for Education Statistics found that 68 percent of homeschoolers were white, 15 percent identified as Hispanic, 8 percent were Black, 4 percent were Asian/Pacific Islander, and 5 percent identified as other.[50]

The heroes of homeschooling are the anarchist intellectual Paul Goodman, who lived and wrote in the mid-twentieth century; John Holt, an educator and the author of *How Children Fail* (1964), *How Children Learn* (1967), and *Instead of Education: Ways to Help People Do Things Better* (1967) ("The human animal is a learning animal," he wrote, "we like to learn; we are good at it; we don't need to be shown or made to do it. What kills the processes are the people interfering with it or trying to regulate it or control it"); and A. S. Neill, the author of a once influential but largely forgotten book called *Summerhill*, about a boarding school run entirely by the students. As a teacher in the

50   Sarah D. Sparks, "NCES Releases Details on Homeschooling," *Education Week*, August 30, 2013, blogs.edweek.org.

1920s, Neill showed no interest in lesson quality or student engagement; his teaching in practice was described as "simply awful" and "incoherent."[51]

In an essay on the movement to allow children to educate themselves independently, called alternatively "unschooling" or "free-range parenting," Astra Taylor, a child raised in an "unschooling" family who found success as a filmmaker, argues that American schooling should learn from radical pedagogy, the willingness "to take seriously words like 'freedom,' 'autonomy,' and 'choice,'" which have been ceded to the political right. Looking "at the radical margins may help us ask better questions about what we really want from our educational system and how to go about getting it."[52] The desperation here is representative of a strong critique of public education. About 3 percent of the school-age population was homeschooled during the 2011–12 school year, the most recent year for which data is available, and by far the most significant reason cited by parents for the decision was concern about school environment.[53]

These are questions worth asking in the golden age of young adult dystopian fiction: Are schools jails? Is institutionalization an inevitably soul-crushing enterprise, meant to inculcate children into, in Taylor's words, an ethos of

51   Richard Bailey, *A. S. Neill* (New York: Bloomsbury, 2014).

52   Astra Taylor, "Learning in Freedom," *n+1*, February 21, 2012, nplusonemag.com.

53   U.S. Department of Education, National Center for Education Statistics, *Parent and Family Involvement in Education, From the National Household Education Surveys Program of 2012* (NCES 2013-028); and U.S. Department of Education, National Center for Education Statistics, *The Condition of Education 2009* (NCES 2009-081), Indicator 6.

boredom? Must we reject the state altogether to change the way children experience education?

The fundamental problem with unschooling is that it fails to account for the fact that privilege and authority, though intimately linked, are not the same thing. It is not only possible but preferable for teachers to guide children without "molding" or forcing them. Goodman and Holt were both committed to delaying socialization in children, regarding growth as an individual, solitary, and natural pursuit that must be protected from the corrupting influence of adults. It's a primitivist impulse. It's also sentimental and paternalistic.

Insistent as these critiques are on the primacy of individual freedom, they almost always invoke self-guided learning as a liberating answer to the oppressive teacher-student relationship. The idea is that, as Goodman wrote, "natural" learning means that the organism itself must create its own structures as it goes. One common refrain is "You don't need to teach a baby how to speak. You speak to it and it learns to speak"— in other words, let nature do her work, and everything will turn out fine.

But it doesn't always turn out fine. Inquiry and engagement are important, but students also need scaffolding, in the form of "modeling, direct teaching, and prompting, which is gradually removed as students become adept at self-evaluation and metacognition."[54] Teachers use direct

---

54 Lauren B. Resnick and Megan Williams Hall, *Principles of Learning for Effort-based Education* (Pittsburgh: University of Pittsburgh, 2003), northeastelementary.org.

instruction strategies not just to bore kids, but because they work: A combination of direct instruction and real-life examples is a more effective way to teach than either is on its own.

Taylor writes,

> Our solitude, to paraphrase Thoreau, was not trespassed upon. What a gift! What kind of respect for intellectual or artistic immersion is signaled by a world in which the sound of a bell means that the work at hand, no matter how compelling or urgent, must be put aside, and something else started? How deeply can anyone enter a subject in fifty minutes unless the material is broken down into component parts too small to communicate any grand purpose?[55]

I read this as a refutation of worksheets. Fine: Who doesn't hate outlines and graphic organizers? Before I began teaching, I promised myself I'd never go near a photocopier. Compare/contrast exercises feel reductive, mechanistic, too "Another Brick in the Wall." But it turns out that this breaking down into component parts is exactly what many students need in order to get to the grand purpose. Study after study has shown that students' ability to identify the structure of a text influences whether or not they understand and remember what they have read. One researcher found that only 11 percent of ninth-graders consciously identified and used high-level structure to recall their reading, and this group

---

55   Astra Taylor, "Unschooling," *n+1*, no. 13 (Winter 2012).

was able to recall twice as much as the students who did not use the strategy.[56] Training the other 89 percent to identify and use top-level structure more than doubled their recall performance.

The ability to recall what you have read matters a lot. The brain's working memory capacity is limited, and if it's entirely devoted to decoding a sentence, it's less likely to be able to construct and engage with meaning. This is why we have to spend years learning basic math before we get to calculus. What separates experts from novices is not some innate mystical genius; it's the fluency and pattern recognition that comes only from hours of practice. Sometimes, learning feels like work because it is work, but not because it's busy work.

There's another aspect of the argument for unschooling in Goodman and Holt that I find troubling. Why shouldn't kids be asked to put away their crayons and go to lunch at the same time? Why do we assume that clear boundaries, a schedule, and a sense of hierarchy are so threatening to students? Why must the individual's vision be so carefully and serenely sheltered from other people, who are experienced in this framework as interruptions? There is value in being pulled out of a daydream. There is value in learning to cope with a little coercion, in knowing what it means to cooperate on a daily basis with someone who doesn't love you, someone who's not your family member.

---

56   Bonnie J. F. Meyer, Carole J. Young, and Brendan J. Bartlett, *Memory Improved: Reading and Memory Enhancement across the Life Span through Strategic Text Structures* (New York: Psychology Press, 2014).

Taylor has summarized the debate over compulsory schooling as "Do we trust people's capacity to be curious or not?" To me, it seems to be about sparing children the discomfort of conflict. Curiosity leads us to follow our own interests, but what about the interests of others? Conflict is what happens when we're asked to reckon with them. Just as not every child learns to read "when they're ready," some students understandably "resist the critical thinking process; they are more comfortable with learning that allows them to remain passive" (as the feminist teacher bell hooks writes in *Teaching Critical Thinking: Practical Wisdom*[57]).

Whether we're willing to admit it or not, there is a body of mainstream academic knowledge that students either have access to or don't—for example, the ability to speak "Standard English"—but which is crucial to being able to support oneself as an adult. In *Other People's Children*, the educator Lisa Delpit writes about her disillusionment with her progressive, child-centered teacher training: "In many African-American communities, teachers are expected to show that they care about their students by controlling the class; exhibiting personal power," and "'pushing' students to achieve."[58] Teachers who don't exhibit these behaviors are regarded as uncaring.

"There are several reasons why students and parents of color take a position that differs from the well-intentioned position of the teachers I have described," she writes.

---

57   bell hooks, *Teaching Critical Thinking: Practical Wisdom* (New York: Routledge, 2009).
58   Lisa Delpit, *Other People's Children: Cultural Conflict in the Classroom* (New York: New Press, 2006), 36.

First, they know that members of society need access to dominant discourses to (legally) have access to economic power. Second, they know that such discourses can be and have been acquired in classrooms because they know individuals who have done so.[59]

Delpit sees the public schools as a place where students should be acquiring the skills and language that help them survive and transform what systemic oppression they will face.

At the heart of the anarchist vision for public schooling is the idea that if public schools don't work for you, you should stop going. Burn them down; refuse to pay taxes. Rebelling against the institutional part of public institutions is the defining characteristic of this response to structural inequality. Goodman sees schooling as social control, the individual thwarted, taxes squandered on "war, school teachers, and politicians." True, education systems have in many cases throughout history served to reinforce the class structures of the society that set them up. But tearing them down or boycotting them and rebuilding on a local level is not a viable solution.

The fact is, we don't need more decentralization in our public schools. US schools are highly decentralized. Liberals and conservatives have long resisted the creation of a national curriculum, effectively handing the power over to Texas and California to create a de facto national curriculum because

59   Ibid., 162.

they order the most textbooks. In 2010, the Texas Board of Education approved a social studies curriculum that emphasizes the importance of capitalism in American life. Board members were unable to agree on whether Darwin's theory of evolution should be included.

It's no accident that this is a microcosm of what is happening to public schools, where parents and kids are increasingly being asked to pitch in and paint the building or hawk candy bars to fill budget gaps. That's because the values of freedom, autonomy, and choice are in perfect accordance with market-based "reforms," and with the neoliberal vision of society on which they're based. In order to resist privatization, we must also resist neoliberalism's tendency to atomize society and force us to compete against each other for limited resources, rather than as empathetic human beings capable of communication, creativity, and solidarity. Alternative, student-centered education sounds like community action, until you remember we're already paying for public schools, and patching them up after hours is an inadequate and piecemeal way to go about changing them. We need a common space that offers students access to knowledge they aren't necessarily getting at home—and we need to insist, through taxation, that the wealthy contribute to it.

Further, while schools in capitalist America undeniably reproduce inequality in ways that are both obvious—tracking and discipline, which are heavily stratified by class background—and more subtle, for example the shaping of children's attitudes and personalities (which the Marxist sociologists Gintis and Bowles documented and categorized), schools should not be underestimated as a place to organize, subvert, and challenge the economic system.

The Sudbury Valley School, founded by Daniel Greenberg in 1968 in Framingham, Massachusetts, is located on a ten-acre campus featuring a millpond, barn, and old stone mansion. Greenberg cites A. S. Neill's *Summerhill* and the works of John Holt as inspiration for the pedagogical foundation of the school, in which kids are given complete freedom over their own day-to-day choices. There are no tests, no curriculum, and no requirements for graduating other than "demonstrating that you will be a productive American citizen."

Developmental psychologist Peter Gray calls it "the best-kept secret in American education."[60] It would seem so. Sudbury has an open admissions policy, accepting students on a first-come, first-serve basis, but no policy for ensuring that information about the school reaches all parents (thus benefiting those with time for research and networking). When I asked the school about race and class demographics, the admissions office told me that they don't keep track of those numbers.

Second, rejecting schooling in general, as a concept, rather than schooling as it exists, allows these critics to imagine easily that they stand with the oppressed, while neglecting the very specific and real oppression in today's schools. A student who has gone through public schooling in Palo Alto

---

60 Peter Gray, *Free to Learn: Why Unleashing the Instinct to Play Will Make Our Children Happier, More Self-reliant, and Better Students for Life* (New York: Basic Books, 2013).

may imagine that her objection to her teacher's authority is the same as the objection of a poor student to her (often middle-class) teacher's authority. It is not. The anarchist critique of schooling is centered on undermining—destroying, actually—the power of teachers, presuming that the presently lopsided power dynamic between teachers and students is the problem.

To continue the previous example, a book published by the Sudbury Valley School, *The Crisis in American Education: An Analysis and A Proposal*, argues that "the educational system in our country today is the most un-American institution we have in our midst," because democracy means that everyone should have equal opportunities and rights, while students do not. Greenberg and his colleagues explicitly link their ideas for schooling to free-market capitalism, with the argument that a democratic school should be "a free marketplace of ideas, a free enterprise system of talents."[61]

As Lisa Delpit has pointed out, this is a distinctly middle-class value, mistaken by radical homeschoolers for a revolutionary agenda.

The state is present, even in underfunded schools, when kids are jailed for "disruption of a school function," for cursing at a teacher, or charged with battery for throwing spitballs. It's present when principals are dismissed for attending a forum that questions the effectiveness of charter schools (which happened in New Jersey in 2013) or when schools

---

61   The Sudbury Valley School, *The Crisis in American Education: An Analysis and A Proposal*, sudval.org; taconicarts.com/projects/sudbury/05_onli_15.html.

close without letting parents know what's going on. And it's present in workplaces in the form of right-to-work laws that inhibit employees from organizing to demand reasonable accommodations for child care—or when, in extreme cases, low-income families are punished by the Administration for Children's Services for not being able to provide their children with the essentials. The question is not whether the state be involved in education—it is, inextricably: Who will control it?

Tearing down our public spaces is not victory. It's a capitulation. Lack of affordable child care already undermines economic security for low-income families, who make considerable financial sacrifices to obtain it. The average salary of a child-care worker is approximately $20,000 a year—the average cost of private center-based child care ranges from about $15,000 (in the South) to $20,000 (in the Northeast) per child annually. As one domestic worker told researcher Bonnie Thorton Dill, without public child-care options, "We have to leave our children; sometimes leave the children alone. There's times when I have asked winos to look after my children."[62]

Why join corporate reformers in supporting the privatization of education and child care? Why not close private schools instead, and force the wealthy to buy in to public education? Rather than middle- and upper-class families

62 Bonnie Thornton Dill, "Race, Class, and Gender: Prospects for an All-Inclusive Sisterhood," in *The Intersectional Approach: Transforming the Academy through Race, Class and Gender*, eds. Michele Tracy Berger and Kathleen Guidroz (Chapel Hill, NC: University of North Carolina Press, 2009).

scrapping together a workable solution, everyone partici-
pates in the same system. This would transform the quality of
public education while leaving open the possibility of public
schools as shared spaces, with equal access to education for
rich and poor. The fact is, we need a common space that
offers students access to knowledge they may be but aren't
necessarily getting at home—and we need to insist, through
taxation, that the wealthy contribute to it.

What would schools based on equal access to resources,
rather than competition for resources, look like? A lot like the
well-rounded curriculum of the private schools and suburban
schools attended by the children of the rich, whose achievement consistently keeps pace with their international peers.
These are schools, like Sidwell Friends (which the Obama
children attend), with small class sizes and an emphasis on
experiential learning and close, individual attention, as well
as creative work.

Feminist sociologist Michèle Barrett has pointed out: "The
state is not a pre-given instrument of oppression, but is a site
of struggle and to some extent at least responsive to concerted
pressure." This pressure won't bring about liberation or
emancipation on its own, but rejecting it altogether is to
"lapse into the romance of anarchism," as she writes.[63] Barrett
is writing in opposition to Althusser's mechanistic argument
that "some apparatuses of the state function primarily by
repression (the army, the police)" and others "primarily by

---

63   Michèle Barrett, *Women's Oppression Today: The Marxist/Feminist
Encounter*, rev. ed. (London: Verso, 1988).

ideology (the educational system, the family, the law, the political system, trade-union institutions, communications, and cultural institutions)," with zero space in between. Althusser saw schools as places where children were indoctrinated into ruling-class ideology. I believe, with Barrett, that the education system is defined by struggle and serves an in-between role, in service of those who seize control over it.

Human beings, whether they are children or adults, resist authority and oppression. Schools are already contested and public sites of resistance for the working class and have been treated as such throughout history. Working-class families have fought for and against public schools and will continue to do so, as they should. In the future, the state can be a powerful instrument for creating child care and education that is liberating, not just oppressive. That will involve committed struggle against the institution of the traditional family, which is presently in competition with other families. It will require solidarity that extends beyond the bounds of the nuclear family.

It's critical work. American public schools have been rapidly resegregating by race and class since the 1990s, with far-reaching consequences, not just for children, but for the entire American working class. In the next chapter, I'll discuss how we got here.

2

A NATION AT RISK? THE POLICY
LANDSCAPE OF PUBLIC EDUCATION

Our Nation is at risk. Our once unchallenged preeminence in commerce, industry, science, and technological innovation is being overtaken by competitors throughout the world. This report is concerned with only one of the many causes and dimensions of the problem, but it is the one that undergirds American prosperity, security, and civility. We report to the American people that while we can take justifiable pride in what our schools and colleges have historically accomplished and contributed to the United States and the well-being of its people, the educational foundations of our society are presently being eroded by a rising tide of mediocrity that threatens our very future as a Nation and a people. What was unimaginable a generation ago has begun to occur—others are matching and surpassing our educational attainments.

If an unfriendly foreign power had attempted to impose on America the mediocre educational performance that exists today, we might well have viewed it as an act of war. As it stands, we

have allowed this to happen to ourselves. We have even squan-
dered the gains in student achievement made in the wake of the
Sputnik challenge. Moreover, we have dismantled essential
support systems which helped make those gains possible. We
have, in effect, been committing an act of unthinking, unilateral
educational disarmament.

—A Nation at Risk, 1983

In 2014, Harvard Business School partnered with the largest
private foundation in the world and one of the world's three
largest management consulting firms to release *A Business*
Leader's Playbook for Supporting America's Schools. The nation's
education system is at a crossroads, they write—"as students
in other countries, both developed and developing, match and
surpass U.S. students, the future dims for our youth and for our
nation's economic competiveness."[1] To indicate the gravity of
the situation, the authors resurrect a warning about "a rising
tide of mediocrity" threatening American society from a three-
decades-old report linking the nation's security and economic
well-being with standardized test results.

They direct business leaders to end "checkbook philanthropy" and start taking transformative actions to change
public schools, including advocating for policies, "(e.g.,
standards, accountability, and choice)," that "enable innovation." That standards, accountability, and choice are rolled

---

1   Jan Rivkin et al., *Lasting Impact: A Business Leader's Playbook for*
Supporting America's Schools (Boston: Harvard Business School, November
2013), hbs.edu.

off parenthetically with a casual "e.g." shows the extent to
which this specific set of market-inspired principles has
become a comprehensive and unified agenda for education
reform.

It wasn't always that way. Though it's hardly ever referenced so directly today, *A Nation at Risk* radically reset the
terms of debate about public schooling in America and
underpins many of the assumptions we now hear about public
schools. It "helped generate education reforms at all levels of
government and propelled the business community to deepen
and expand its role in improving educational outcomes from
students," according to ed.gov, the US Department of
Education website, in a press release announcing that US
Secretary of Education Arne Duncan would be celebrating
the thirtieth anniversary of the report's release by addressing
fifty CEOs.[2]

In 1981, the year Reagan was elected to his first term, the
GOP's educational agenda consisted of two main objectives:
"Bring God back into the classroom" and abolish the
Department of Education. This put the Reagan-appointed
secretary of education, Terrel Bell, in an awkward position.
Pressured to dismantle the very organization he'd been
chosen to oversee, Bell instead assembled a task force, the
National Commission on Excellence in Education (NCEE),
to look critically at data that had been collected by the
Department of Education but never released. "I wanted to

---

2 "Education Secretary Arne Duncan to Address Business Coalition
for Student Achievement on 30th Anniversary of *A Nation at Risk*," US
Department of Education, ed.gov.

stage an event that would jar the people into action on behalf of their educational system," Bell has written in his autobiography.[3]

In April 1983, the NCEE released *A Nation at Risk: The Imperative for Educational Reform*—the most influential document on education policy since Congress passed Title I of the Elementary and Secondary Education Act in 1965, a compensatory reform that provided federal funds for the education of children of low-income families. But where Title I took an equalizing approach to reform, allocating funds specifically to districts with a high share of students from low-income families, *A Nation at Risk* called for higher expectations for all students, regardless of socioeconomic status: "We must demand the best effort and performance from all students, whether they are gifted or less able, affluent or disadvantaged, whether destined for college, the farm, or industry."

At the time of the report's release, Americans were—as Bell recalls—fraught with anxiety over job loss, inflation, international industrial competition, and a perceived decline in prestige due to the hostage crisis in Iran. Education ranked low on the list of national priorities. So the NCEE used the language of warfare to conflate what was supposedly a crisis in public schools with a crisis in national security.

The problem, as they saw it, was that kids were graduating from high school unprepared for success in a global

---

3   Terrel H. Bell, *The Thirteenth Man: A Reagan Cabinet Memoir* (New York: Free Press, 1988).

economy. Their solution was more effort, with an emphasis on the advancement of students' personal, educational, and occupational goals. A list of action items to be implemented immediately included: performance-based salaries for teachers, the use of standardized tests for evaluation, grade placement determined by progress rather than by age, the shuttling of disruptive students to alternative schools, increased homework load, attendance policies with incentives and sanctions, and the extension of the school day—in other words, longer, harder hours.

Every one of these ideas is rooted in the free-market ideology of business. For the first time since Sputnik (when American elites began to panic about capitalism "falling behind" communism technologically), the role of the public schools had been reimagined as a kind of baptism by fire into the competitive world of adulthood. Teachers and children would be expected to produce results or face punitive measures—pressures typically experienced in industrial workplaces, not classrooms. Kids would learn, not for the joy of it, not because of democratic zeal for a literate citizenry, and not even because it was good for them, like taking vitamins—but to keep America globally competitive.

In a highly publicized press conference following the report's release on April 26, Reagan was forced to do an about-face on his fervent insistence that the federal government stay out of public education: "We're entering a new era and education holds the key," he said to reporters.

Rather than fear our future, let us embrace it and make it work for us by improving instruction in science and math, retraining our workers, encouraging their continued education, retooling our factories and stimulating investment in new areas of growth. We can do that. We can compete and meet the challenges of the marketplace. We're still the world's technological leader, but to be stronger, we have to get smart. America needs more education power.[4]

That day, the headline in the *New York Times* was "Commission on Education Warns 'Rising Tide of Mediocrity' Imperils U.S."[5]

The next day, the paper's education editor interviewed William O. Baker, chairman of the board of Bell Telephone and a member of the National Commission on Excellence in Education, who repeated the demands in the report: "The current situation is intolerable. We're saying to the country: Get with it. Do something about it." The same article noted major errors in the commission's evidence, most concretely, the statement that College Board achievement tests "reveal consistent declines in recent years in such subjects as physics and English"—which a spokesman for the College Board told the *Times* was incorrect.[6] It pointed to widely published data the commission had not addressed that showed that the

<hr />

4 "Public Papers of the Presidents of the United States: Ronald Reagan," 1983, 586.

5 Edward B. Fiske, "Commission on Education Warns 'Tide of Mediocrity' Imperils U.S.," *New York Times*, April 27, 1983, nytimes.com.

6 Edward B. Fiske, "Problem for Education; News Analysis," *New York Times*, April 28, 1983, nytimes.com.

performance of elementary and junior high students had improved on state tests since the mid-1970s. Baker's response? "We disregarded what we didn't believe."

A Nation at Risk contains zero citations, making its claims difficult to verify. Two sociologists of education, David Berliner and Bruce Biddle, have argued that a main point on which the authors based their recommendations—that SAT scores had steadily declined since the 1960s—was actually a misinterpretation of the data: As a voluntary test taken by those intending to go to college, the SAT should never have been aggregated to evaluate the quality of teachers or schools.[7] The slight drop in test scores interpreted by the commission to mean that America's schools (and its prosperity, security, and civility) were spiraling downward actually reflected the fact that a growing number of people from a diversity of backgrounds, including immigrants and beneficiaries of the GI Bill, had ambitions to go to college and were taking the test. For example, whereas in 1970, only 57 percent of white adults and 36 percent of Black adults had finished high school, 94 percent of white adults and 88 percent of Black adults had by 1998.

When the data is disaggregated, or broken down by socioeconomic status, race and ethnicity, and ESL status, it shows that math scores for all groups during the years preceding the release of the report increased, while verbal scores remained constant. Far from representing a decrease in academic

---

7   David C. Berliner and Bruce J. Biddle, *The Manufactured Crisis* (Reading, MA: Addison-Wesley, 1995).

excellence, the evidence points to an increased interest in higher education among those not traditionally embraced by academia, i.e., nonwhite males.[8]

Linda Darling-Hammond, an education policy scholar and founder of the Stanford Center for Opportunity Policy in Education, has observed that SAT scores for students of color rose sharply after 1970 even though more students took the test. Likewise, twelfth-graders' scores on the National Assessment of Educational Progress or NAEP, a much more holistic battery of tests known as "the Nation's Report Card," have changed little over the past several decades, "even though a great many more educationally disadvantaged students—including special education students, new immigrants and English-language learners, students living in poverty, and students of color—now reach the twelfth grade and are part of the testing pool." She explained, "The fact that their inclusion has not lowered the average is a sign that, for most students," performance on standardized tests has actually improved.[9]

Of course, *A Nation at Risk* wasn't influential because it was accurate. It was influential because it was the version of events that American voters and policy makers wanted to believe at the time. It had the convenient effect of converting what had been a material crisis into a struggle for the soul of American schools, a material problem into a deficiency of

8   Ibid.
9   Linda Darling-Hammond, "Inequality and School Resources: What It Will Take to Close the Opportunity Gap," in *Closing the Opportunity Gap: What America Must Do to Give Every Child an Even Chance*, eds. Prudence L. Carter and Kevin G. Welner (New York: Oxford University Press, 2013), 93.

gumption. Its tantalizingly simplistic implication was that social problems arise not from a specific set of policies and realities—segregation, discrimination, poverty—but from a lack of willpower: the malaise hinted at in *A Nation At Risk*. If a poor kid couldn't succeed, she just didn't have the right attitude. That is not an overstatement—it is the central assumption that animates every initiative we gather together and call education reform.

The incorporation of free-market language in the report was a nod to Reagan, and it gave him reason enough to embrace it, which he did, a year later—taking credit for having assembled the commission in his State of the Union Address the following year.

In 1984, a *New York Times* editorial asserted that the report had been *revolutionary*. "It started a groundswell movement calling for increased standards and implementation of other reforms to change dramatically the performance of our schools," including inviting private industry "to take a more active role in supporting and improving" schools. "We are witnessing a tidal wave of reform, unprecedented in its breadth and support, that promises to restore excellence as the hallmark of American education," the paper concluded.[10] The conventional wisdom that schools were in crisis was now accepted as fact.

Four years later, Congress's reauthorization of the Elementary and Secondary Education Act, or ESEA (the bill

10   "On the Record; Bell on Educational Gains," *New York Times*, April 28, 1984, nytimes.com.

that provides federal funding to American public schools), required for the first time that states "define the levels of academic achievement that poor students should attain" and "identify schools in which students were not achieving as expected." George H. W. Bush, Reagan's Republican successor, campaigned in 1988 to be the "education president," an issue the Republicans had previously been happy to let the Democrats own.

In his memoir, Bell noted that the "high political payoff" of *A Nation at Risk* "stole the education issue from Walter Mondale—and it cost us nothing."[11] It's an assessment that rings true of the entire circus. A great deal of politicking was done, and public sentiment was changed almost overnight; but ultimately, the way schools are organized and funded remained the same. The difference was the slow but significant ideological shift from emphasizing equity and the rights of historically oppressed groups to an emphasis on excellence and achievement for "all" students, which persists today.

In a short film directed by Joe Portnoy, special assistant for digital and visual media at the US Department of Education, and created by the American Enterprise Institute for the thirtieth anniversary of *A Nation at Risk*, Secretary of Education Arne Duncan credits the task force that produced the report with "challenging us to figure out 'how do we maximize our resources to achieve the systemic change we need?'" He concludes that there's still "a lack of urgency, that we continue

---

11   Bell, *The Thirteenth Man*, 155.

to fight. As much as they thought that thirty years ago, I still feel that today."[12]

Secular, free, and (in theory) universal, the American "common school"—the first free, publicly supported school system in the country, established during the nineteenth century—was inspired by the same Protestantism and Enlightenment liberal ethics as its political system. Education is "the great equalizer of the conditions of men— the balance wheel of the social machinery," wrote Horace Mann, the founding "father" of the common school movement, in 1848.[13] Equality is understood and articulated as a goal to be achieved by spreading opportunity. Attachment to this meritocratic ideal has led intellectual elites and the voting public alike to treat American public schools as a social safety net, grafting Gilded Age fantasies about lifting oneself up by one's bootstraps and Cold War anxieties about losing the technological arms race[14] onto the education system.[15]

---

12 *A Nation at Risk: 30 Years Later* (2013), dir. Joe Portnoy, prod. American Enterprise Institute, aei.org.

13 Roslin Growe and Paula S. Montgomery, "Educational Equity in America: Is Education the Great Equalizer?," *Professional Educator* 25, no. 2 (2003).

14 John E. Sununu and Maria Cardona, "STEM Fund Key to Global Competitiveness," *Congress Blog, The Hill*, June 12, 2013, thehill.com.

15 See, for example, David Rohde, Kristina Cooke, and Himanshu Ojha, "The Decline of the 'Great Equalizer,'" *Atlantic*, December 19, 2012, theatlantic.com, about education and rising inequality; and Douglas B. Downey, Paul T. von Hippel, and Beckett A. Broh, "Are Schools the Great Equalizer? Cognitive Inequality during the Summer Months and the School Year," *American Sociological Review* 69, no. 5 (October 2004): 613–35, asr. sagepub.com.

It makes sense then, that as mainstream attitudes toward the problems of the country's growing lower class changed in the 1980s, the way policy makers and academics talked about the problems facing the nation's schools also changed.

During the late 1980s and 1990s, prominent advocates of choice policies and school privatization constructed a forceful intellectual argument that the social justice movements and Great Society programs of the previous decades had produced bureaucratic educational "entitlements" benefiting special interests, while failing mainstream and "gifted" children.

In 1990, Reagan's assistant secretary of education, Chester E. Finn, called Terry Moe and John Chubb's *Politics, Markets and America's Schools* "the most eagerly awaited book of the year." He was right. Enormously influential on politicians and education "reform" activists alike, it is a foundational text for the standards and accountability movement in America, making the case that the education system should be run according to market principles.

In it, Chubb and Moe, fellows at the Brookings Institution and Stanford's Hoover Institution respectively, theorize that poor performance is "one of the prices Americans pay for choosing to exercise democratic control over their schools."[16] Even the most sweeping reforms of the school system are destined to fail, they argue, because declining academic performance is not due to problems *within* American public schools, but to the very nature of the schools themselves as

---

16 John E. Chubb and Terry M. Moe, "The Root of the Problem," in *Politics, Markets and America's Schools* (Washington, DC: Brookings Institution Press, 1990), 1–25.

"institutions of direct democratic control," which, they observed, "appear incompatible with effective schooling."

They look back longingly to the 1950s, when the launch of Sputnik sent "shock waves" through the educational community and ignited "frenzied concern" among the public that America was losing the space race and endangering its national security because of a lack of demanding training in technical subjects—until the counterculture ushered in what they characterize as "loose or non-existent standards" for kids in public schools:

> The issue of academic excellence then rather quickly plummeted on the national agenda, to be superseded by others—notably, race and equal opportunity—that, by no coincidence, were closely bound up with the broader social controversies that animated the turbulent politics of the 1960s and 1970s. Meantime, there was no indication that the schools had actually improved. The problem of academic excellence remained.

It is critical to note that at the time that Chubb and Moe were writing, American schools were at their *highest ever* level of Black-white desegregation—integration peaked between 1980 and 1988, then steadily declined when the Supreme Court allowed desegregation plans to be terminated.[17] Further, during the 1970s and 1980s, there were

---

17   Sarah Childress, "Report: School Segregation Is Back, 60 Years after 'Brown,'" *Frontline*, May 15, 2014, pbs.org.

substantial reductions in the "achievement gap" between white students and Black students as reported on the NAEP at the same time that the national average class size was decreasing.[18] The implicit and enduring suggestion is that academic excellence is in opposition to "race and equal opportunity," as if attention to one detracts from the other (which it does not).

Ironically, while they express alienation with the progressive 1960s and 70s and their focus on equity, race, and desegregation, and insist that the corporation should be the model for the schools of the future (since it has a "genuine" methodological interest in "discovering the true causes of poor educational performance"), Chubb and Moe appropriate the critique of centralization and struggle for community control from the Black Power and other progressive education reform movements of that era and rearticulate it as a rationale for traditional parental authority and systematic privatization of the public schools.

Until the twentieth century, they write, education was in the hands of parents and local communities and concerned with "simple, important things that ordinary people cared about and could understand." People imagined

that they could and should be able to govern their own educational affairs. And as they proceeded—all across America, without plan or coordination—to fashion the

18   Paul E. Barton and Richard J. Coley, *The Black-White Achievement Gap: When Progress Stopped*, Policy Information Report (Princeton, NJ: Educational Testing Service, July 2010), ets.org.

kinds of schools they wanted for themselves and their children, the great heterogeneity of the nation came to be reflected in the diversity and autonomy of its local schools.

Never mind that the kinds of schools Americans fashioned frequently involved institutionalized segregation and violence for children from poor families, Black children, Mexican American children, and Native American children, accumulating over time into what the distinguished pedagogical theorist Gloria Ladson-Billings has called an "education debt."[19] Or that nineteenth-century "charity schools" were dependent on and shaped ideologically by the inclinations of rich white donors obsessed with the moral instruction of the poor rather than with providing universal high-quality education.[20] (Charity schooling, which existed as an alternative for those who could not afford private school prior to the widespread adoption of the common school in the early 1900s, provided, at best, some amelioration of the child-care burdens of the working class and, at worst, indicted them as culturally deficient.)

Two years after the book's release, Chubb would go on to found EdisonLearning, an education management company that works with "disadvantaged communities" to "create innovative charter schools, to turn around underperforming public schools and to bring online educational solutions to

19 Gloria Ladson-Billings, "From the Achievement Gap to the Education Debt: Understanding Achievement in U.S. Schools," *Educational Researcher* 35, no. 7 (October 2006): 3–12, edr.sagepub.com.

20 Carl F. Kaestle and Eric Foner, *Pillars of the Republic: Common Schools and American Society, 1780–1860* (New York: Hill and Wang, 1983).

schools and families." Moe's books have been bestsellers, praised by key education reformers from StudentsFirst founder Michelle Rhee to former NYC Schools Chancellor Joel Klein, both staunch advocates of choice reforms in public schooling.

In 1999, the Hoover Institution and Stanford University brought together many of the nation's key standards and accountability advocates from the academic world on the Koret Task Force, which continues to serve as an intellectual backbone for the contemporary education reform movement. Chaired by Finn, its members include Chubb, Moe, Eric Hanushek, and Paul T. Hill, a social scientist who spent seventeen years at the RAND Corporation studying school governance, business-led education reforms, national defense, and military research and development.

In his widely read essay, "The Federal Role in Education," Hill compares the federal government to "ice nine," a fictional liquid dreamed up by Kurt Vonnegut in his novel *Cat's Cradle*, which kills people instantly on contact. The government is, he insists, outdated, coercive, and bureaucratic, exerting a "colonizing" influence on intimate community assets to *force* the equal use of state and local funds. He argues that the weaknesses of American schools can be attributed to their "forced adoption" of attributes common to regulated industries during the Johnson administration, and that government interference in measuring equity in schools has interfered with effective instruction. Just one drop of ice nine, he reminds us, can freeze an ocean. The government has done what it does best, he says, by redistributing opportunities—an assertion that was and is categorically untrue—now it's time to "create intimate, imaginative, highly productive institutions." "Laws that create absolute entitlements to specific services or permit court orders requiring optimal services for some children regardless of the consequences for other children's education must be amended," he writes euphemistically.[21] Who are these children receiving "optimal services" and entitlements, and who are the children whose education is being sacrificed to do so? Given his invocation of *Brown v. Board of Ed.* and the 1960s and 70s, the height of progressivism and integration in American public education, it's hard to read his statement as anything but the thinly veiled suggestion that a focus on expanding equity for poor and minority children has come at the expense of excellence for "all," meaning white, middle-class children.

In the tradition of Chubb and Moe, Hill draws on the language of "community" and freedom from colonization to advance a deeply conservative agenda. Hill's ideal model is not the corporation but the private Catholic school, which, he argues, holds children to higher standards than public schools and responds to their differences as "temporary impediments to the student's learning the knowledge, skills, and habits that the school intends to impart to all students," rather than dividing them into the K–12 equivalent of special interest groups.[22]

---

21   Paul T. Hill, "The Federal Role in Education," *Brookings Papers on Education Policy* 3 (2000): 11–57.
22   Ibid.

"Educational choice means that parents are given back a basic American ideal of freedom to choose as it applies to the education of their children," reads the mission statement of the Milton and Rose D. Friedman Foundation.[23] "Yes, given back, for America's system was not founded in public education." The foundation is a self-proclaimed resource for parents and "community groups who want parent choice in education, and are ready to fight for it."

In fact, researchers have shown that when public school choice is available, highly educated parents are especially likely to factor student demographics in the selection of a school for their child.[24] The authors of a 2009 study on school choice found results consistent with earlier research showing that "privileged families use choice policies to opt out of public schools with greater concentrations" of "economically disadvantaged students."[25] And Black-white segregation has tended to increase substantially without court oversight.[26] Today's schools are more segregated by race than they were in 1968, with Blacks and Latinos typically attending schools with two times the level of poverty as whites and Asians,

23   Walter Feinberg and Christopher Lubienski, eds., *School Choice Policies and Outcomes: Empirical and Philosophical Perspectives* (Albany, NY: SUNY Press, 2008), 63.

24   Jennifer L. Hochschild and Nathan Scovronick, *The American Dream and the Public Schools* (New York: Oxford University Press, 2003).

25   Jack Dougherty et al., "School Information, Parental Decisions, and the Digital Divide: The SmartChoices Project in Hartford, Connecticut," in *Educational Delusions?: Why Choice Can Deepen Inequality and How to Make Schools Fair*, eds. Erica Frankenberg and Gary Orfield, (Berkeley, CA: University of California Press, 2012), 235.

26   Jason M. Breslow, Evan Wexler, and Robert Collins, "The Return of School Segregation in Eight Charts," *Frontline*, July 15, 2014, pbs.org.

according to Gary Orfield of the UCLA Civil Rights Project.[27] In some districts and states, charter schools even serve as "havens for white flight"—for example, one study found that nearly 70 percent of Delaware's charter schools enroll either 70 percent or more white students, or almost none.[28] This negatively impacts public schools: In spring 2012, Philadelphia announced that due to budget cuts and high charter enrollment, it would disband in 2017.[29] This is a particularly perverse development given that many charter networks, such as KIPP, are completely underwritten by philanthropic donations.

While "choice" advocates argue that charter schools and voucher programs benefit economically disadvantaged families by making schools compete over students and giving parents the freedom to decide where their children are educated, researchers have concluded that schools that control their own admissions "are much less likely to have a proportional share of low-income students than other schools."[30] Why? Charter schools are not required to provide transportation, and low-income families are less likely to have access to their own forms of transportation. They are also less likely to have access to "established social networks through which to discover and research alternative

27   Childress, "Report: School Segregation Is Back."
28   Sarah Butrymowicz, "A New Round of Segregation Plays Out in Charter Schools," *Hechinger Report*, July 15, 2013, hechingerreport.org.
29   Erica Frankenberg and Genevieve Siegel-Hawley, "A Segregating Choice? An Overview of Charter School Policy, Enrollment Trends, and Segregation," in Frankenberg and Orfield, *Educational Delusions?*
30   Hochschild and Scovronick, *The American Dream and the Public Schools*, 116.

options."[31] Meanwhile, a large body of education research has determined that education quality "plunges in schools where the percentage of poor students rises above a particular threshold. Poor students perform better when studying among students who are not poor."[32]

Segregation in American schools is accelerating. In a critical 2007 Supreme Court decision that will have lasting effects on the demographics of public schools, *Parents Involved in Community Schools v. Seattle*, Chief Justice John Roberts declared it "patently unconstitutional" to assign students to schools using racial classifications alone (instead of as one component in assessing diversity) to achieve racial balance, and a divided court ruled that students may not be assigned or denied a school on the basis of race alone, reversing forty years of decisions that allowed or required race to be used as a criteria for student school assignment and effectively dismantling voluntary integration efforts.[33] The same year, education policy researchers Gary Orfield and Chungmei Lee found that resegregation was not only growing nationally, but accelerating in the South, the only region of the United States where schools had ever been highly desegregated.[34] American children "are much poorer than they were

---

31   Ibid.

32   Molly S. McUsic, "The Law's Role in the Distribution of Education: The Promises and Pitfalls of School Finance Litigation," in *Law and School Reform: Six Strategies for Promoting Educational Equity*, ed. Jay P. Heubert (New Haven, CT: Yale University Press, 1999), 88–159.

33   Cara Sandberg, "The Story of *Parents Involved in Community Schools*," student paper, Berkeley Law, University of California, law.berkeley.edu.

34   Gary Orfield and Chungmei Lee, *Historic Reversals, Accelerating*

decades ago and more separated in highly unequal schools,"
they concluded. "Black and Latino segregation is usually
double segregation, both from whites and from middle-class
students. For blacks, more than a third of a century of progress
in racial integration has been lost." For Latinos, they noted,
segregation is more severe than it was in the 1960s. In a study
of metro Boston schools, Orfield and Lee found a strong
correlation between the race and poverty level of students
and the kind of education they experienced: Schools serving
predominantly black and Latino students and high-poverty
schools—there is significant overlap between the categories—are more likely to have inexperienced or unqualified
teachers, high dropout rates, and low scores on high-stakes
state tests.[35]

Even in this environment of intensifying segregation,
charter schools stand out as being far more likely to be
comprised of students from one race than traditional public
schools do. Genevieve Siegel-Hawley and Erica Frankenberg,
former research and policy director at the Civil Rights
Project at UCLA, found that while segregation in public
schools is the highest it's been in two decades, students "of
every racial/ethnic background" are "substantially" *more*
segregated in charter schools than they are in public schools.

Resegregation, and the Need for New Integration Strategies (Los Angeles: Civil
Rights Project/*Proyecto Derechos Civiles*, UCLA, August 2007),
civilrightsproject.ucla.edu. Some districts have attempted to use class as a
proxy for race to increase public school diversity, with varied success.

35   Gary Orfield and Chungmei Lee, *Why Segregation Matters: Poverty
and Educational Inequality* (Cambridge, MA: Civil Rights Project, Harvard
University, January 2005), civilrightsproject.ucla.edu.

While just 15 percent of students attending public schools are in 90 to 100 percent minority schools, almost 60 percent of charter school students are.

It is illegal for charters to discriminate based on race, but there is also very little civil rights legislation that does apply: They are not required to provide services for children with special needs, as public schools are, nor must they hire teachers trained in working with English-language learners.

At issue in this debate is not merely transparency, but power. The most immediate concern raised by education reformers is always: Who controls the schools? But implicit in this undeniably important question is an even more radical set of questions: What *must* people know, and how should they learn it? How should children spend their days? How should their parents and teachers?

The unilateral embrace of school "choice" as an agenda for education reform in the 1990s is among the most bipartisan political reform projects in American history—George H. W. Bush proposed a federally supported voucher program with report cards for school districts, and Bill Clinton "repeatedly stated during the 1992 campaign that 'in a Clinton administration, we will have no higher priority than the improvement of education for every child.'"[36] In 1995, he echoed the national security metaphors of *A Nation at Risk*, comparing "cutting education today" to "cutting defense

36   Patrick J. McGuinn, *No Child Left Behind and the Transformation of Federal Education Policy, 1965–2005* (Lawrence, KS: University Press of Kansas, 2006).

budgets at the height of the Cold War."[37] In 1999, the year the Koret Task Force was founded, he called for 3,000 charter schools to be opened within three years.

Bush unequivocally rejected the antigovernment approach of the Reagan administration; Christopher T. Cross, assistant secretary of education under the first Bush administration, recalls that he gave top CEOs like John Akers, chair of IBM, assignments in specific states, "to work with the governor and other state leaders over the coming decade to help improve the schools."[38] Bush's proposal to reform education, America 2000, focused on expanding parental choice; aimed to provide for the creation of a hybrid public/private "New American Schools Development Corporation" to design model schools; and to promote the publication of report cards for schools, districts, and states as well as voluntary national standards and merit pay and alternative certification for teachers and principals.[39] The proposal went nowhere due to bickering over history standards, but each of its major components was later successfully supported by Clinton and adopted into his own proposal, Goals 2000. After his landslide defeat of Bob Dole—who ran on the traditional Republican platform, including the abolishment of the Department of Education—in 1996, Republicans were so hungry to reclaim the presidency that they abandoned their

---

37 National Archives and Records Administration, Office of the Federal Register, *Public Papers of the Presidents: William J. Clinton, 2005* (Washington, DC: Government Printing Office, 1997), 1060.

38 Christopher T. Cross, *Political Education: National Policy Comes of Age* (New York: Teachers College Press, 2004), 95.

39 Ibid.

fear of federal involvement, and, "by the end of the Clinton presidency, Republicans and Democrats were vying to see who could add the most money to programs like special education."[40]

The culmination of school "choice" as a driving ideology for federal education policy was the reauthorization of the ESEA, originally passed under the Johnson Administration in 1965, as "No Child Left Behind." NCLB, coauthored by Senator Ted Kennedy, a Democrat, and Republican Speaker of the House John Boehner, requires all schools receiving Title I funding to demonstrate through standardized tests that they've achieved adequate yearly progress: In other words, this year's students must perform measurably better on the tests than the last year's group of students. NCLB was signed into law by President George W. Bush in 2002, having succeeded where his father's education proposal, America 2000, had failed. NCLB was backed both by Congressional conservatives—despite the party's long tradition of opposition to national curricular standards and federal spending on public education in general—and by liberal Democrats, who had presided over the largest expansion of *targeted* aid for low-income students in American history just thirty years prior.

NCLB retained the compensatory education model established by ESEA, in which schooling was framed as a way to make up for the deleterious effects of poverty on "disadvantaged" children, but instead of directly allocating money for

40   Ibid., 108.

poor school districts, it emphasized schools' accountability for raising the achievement of *all* students on standardized tests. But as many educational researchers have demonstrated, the crisis of the past twenty-five years has *not* been one of low achievement of *all* students.[41]

NCLB was popular because it gave Democrats an opportunity to parade their commitment to "the civil rights issue of our time" while appearing tough-minded, practical, and solution-oriented. Republican advocates could now lend rhetorical support to public education as a job preparation program and national security issue without being seen as bowing to the pressure of "special interest groups" like teachers' unions, minorities, and those eligible for special education, a critical development for the party given voters' renewed sense of urgency since *A Nation at Risk*. The connections NCLB established between standards-based reforms, educational equity, and marketization was not only useful for political grandstanding but also essential to the successful advancement of the neoliberal agenda—cost cutting, union busting, the infusion of competition, and privatization—in American public schools.

The crux of the legislation is a provision requiring schools appraised as "failing" by state assessments for five consecutive years to "restructure" by firing all staff and/or reorganizing in the form of a charter school, despite no conclusive evidence showing that charter schools outperform traditional

---

41   Berliner and Biddle, *The Manufactured Crisis*; and Hochschild and Scovronick, *The American Dream and the Public Schools*.

schools and plenty of evidence showing that charters increase racial and economic segregation in communities.[42]

In 2011, former Congressman Newt Gingrich suggested that failing schools fire unionized janitors and pay local students to do the work instead. "The kids would actually do work, they would have cash," he said. "They'd begin the process of rising."[43] This may have sounded crass, but it shouldn't be surprising. It is simply a tactless articulation of the market-based mindset—advocating for choice, merit pay, and standardization of assessments and curriculum—that has dominated policy discussions since the 1980s.

The problem, according to Gingrich, is that poor kids just aren't up to the bootstrapping required for success in the free-market economy: "Really poor children in really poor neighborhoods have no habits of working and have nobody around them who works, so they have no habit of showing up on Monday," he said.[44]

Days after Gingrich was excoriated in the *New York Times*, a blogger at the pro-charter Hoover Institution (home of Terry Moe, Michael J. Petrilli, and other choice and privatization advocates) asked, "Is it time for education reformers to pay Gingrich some more attention?" Newt's a goofball,

---

42   Amy Stuart Wells and Jennifer Jellison Holme, "Marketization in Education: Looking Back to Move Forward with a Stronger Critique," in *International Handbook of Educational Policy*, eds. Nina Bascia et al. (London: Springer, 2005), 19–51.

43   Maggie Haberman, "Newt: Fire the Janitors, Hire Kids to Clean Schools," *Politico*, January 1, 2011, politico.com.

44   Charles M. Blow, "Newt's War on Poor Children," *New York Times*, December 2, 2011, nytimes.com.

and an easy target for bleeding-heart liberals, the writer argued, but he's also right.

Under the influence of these reformers, the American education system has become less about curriculum and critical thinking. In public schools across the country, particularly urban ones, social studies and music classes are commonly replaced by the kind of glorified vocational training called for in *A Nation at Risk*. The pro-charter Gates Foundation, which has spent $5 billion dollars on urban education initiatives over the past ten years—including the "small schools" movement, an admitted failure, even by the Gates Foundation[45]—began to advocate that summer internships be made a permanent part of the high school curriculum in 2006. Andrew Carnegie was content to control the building and naming of cultural institutions—the new wave of philanthrocapitalists, with Gates at the forefront, wants a say in what goes on inside them.

The problem is not that business has never before used

---

45   In a 2008 speech at the Forum on Education in America, Bill Gates said, "In the first four years of our work with new, small schools, most of the schools had achievement scores below district averages on reading and math assessments. In one set of schools we supported, graduation rates were no better than the statewide average, and reading and math scores were consistently below the average. The percentage of students attending college the year after graduating high school was up only 2.5 percentage points after five years. Simply breaking up existing schools into smaller units often did not generate the gains we were hoping for." The question is: Why must the students in these schools rely on the hope and intuition of a billionaire for support? Why implement the change in real schools, subjecting real students to the consequences—and only then conclude that the solution doesn't work? The promise of the funds that billionaires will bring to high-poverty schools entices politicians and administrators to enable the same billionaires to use the schools as labs to try out their own ideas, instead of turning to decades of preexisting research.

donations to exact control over government, or that an extraordinary amount is being given. (The Harvard Business School report published in collaboration with the Gates Foundation and the Boston Consulting Group estimates that the business community gives $3 to 4 billion annually to American schools, which in the context of the $632 billion provided through taxation is not much.[46])

The problem is that with donor cash comes a set of beliefs, awkwardly transplanted from the business world to the classroom: the management guru's vision of empowerment as a personal struggle, the CEO's conviction that individual success is limited only by a lack of ambition, life as a series of goals waiting to be met. The type of advice once reserved for dieters, rookie sales associates, and the unemployed is now repeated to public school children with new age fervor: Think positive. Set goals and achieve them. Reach for the stars. Race to the top. It's never too early to network. Just smile.

Like the promise of *A Nation at Risk*, these admonitions are at once wildly idealistic and bitterly cruel—after all, in the (rather violent) words of the report's authors,

> You forfeit your chance for life at its fullest when you withhold your best effort in learning . . . When you work to your full capacity, you can hope to attain the knowledge and skills that will enable you to create your future and

---

46 Rivkin et al., *Lasting Impact*; and "Fast Facts: Expenditures," National Center for Education Statistics, nces.ed.gov.

control your destiny. If you do not, you will have your future thrust upon you by others.

But who will coach you toward your goals? As it happens, this is exactly the kind of thing at which the business community excels. A new genre of nonprofits has been invented solely for the purpose of connecting business leaders with high school principals. For example, the website for PENCIL, one such organization, features pictures of prominent business people (the vice president of human capital management at Goldman Sachs, the CEO of JetBlue) smiling in front of a chalkboard, surrounded by drawings of mountains and spaceships. "See how an airline mogul is encouraging students at Aviation High School to soar. See how a visionary is helping students at P.S. 86K build a greener planet," reads the accompanying text.[47]

The business leader is the ultimate embodiment of success. When you conceive of the schools as a holding pen for grooming tomorrow's talent, it makes sense to turn to him or her for expert counsel. This is exactly the kind of thinking that led former New York City Schools Chancellor Dennis Walcott to plea to the business community for support on PENCIL's behalf. The message to businesses: We need you now more than ever. The for-profit testing industry has risen to provide the instruments of American students' transformation into fearless, proficient, and likable employees.

The most radical change currently underway in American

---

47   pencil.org.

public schools is the reconceptualization of the role of the student-citizen whose education is funded by taxes, to the beneficiary of philanthropic largesse. A press release for the Goldman Sachs Foundation's Next Generation Venture Fund refers paternalistically to "disadvantaged youth" as "undeveloped 'diamonds in the rough,' unprepared for the intense competition for coveted places in higher education and the professional world."[48] The business leader and the education reformer seek to improve the child, because childhood—in the logic of capitalism—is a temporary state of immaturity (productivity) on the way to adulthood, which must be overcome. There are two conditions that students and teachers can feel in response to improvement: self-mastery or gratitude.

There's also a practical reason that public schools are the chosen battlegrounds where corporate reformers seek to spend their time. The student body of today will be the labor force of tomorrow. Businesses have a fierce self-interest in influencing the habits, skills, and attitudes children learn while they are in school because it externalizes the cost of job training onto American taxpayers. As Maryland-based defense firm Lockheed Martin, one of the top five military employers in the country, has stated publicly with regards to their STEM (science, technology, engineering, and math) education grants, "Industry has an important role to play in building the workforce pipeline—and the classroom is the

---

48   Goldman Sachs Foundation Next Generation Venture Fund press release, 2011.

place to begin." Education is "a critical focus for Lockheed Martin. We know firsthand the importance of educating our young people in these areas."[49]

The fact is, there is a way for corporations to contribute to the public welfare already built in to our system: taxation. Like individuals, corporations are theoretically accountable for paying their share of property taxes to American public schools, which comprise over 40 percent of funds for public schooling. Unlike individuals, they do not—naturally, they would rather pay their bill in the form of a donation, and the country's judicial and political systems are happy to comply. In March 2013, the Maryland Senate passed a bill that would exempt Lockheed Martin from paying $450,000 a year in county taxes.

Walmart, the nation's largest private sector employer, avoids an estimated $1 billion in federal taxes annually through the use of tax breaks and loopholes, according to a report by Americans for Tax Fairness. In addition, the corporation benefits directly from $6.2 billion in the form of taxpayer-funded social welfare programs like Medicaid and SNAP—in many states, Walmart employees are the largest group of recipients of both programs, receiving an average of $1,000 in aid, meaning taxpayers effectively subsidize the company's poverty-level wages.[50] The Walton Family

---

49   "STEM Education," lockheedmartin.com.

50   Americans for Tax Fairness, *Walmart on Tax Day: How Taxpayers Subsidize America's Biggest Employer and Richest Family* (Washington, DC: Americans for Tax Fairness, April 2014), americansfortaxfairness.org; and Tim Worstall, "Apologies, but Welfare Payments to Employees Are Not Subsidies to Walmart and McDonalds," *Forbes*, November 13, 2013, forbes. com.

Foundation is one of the most prominent supporters of corporate education reform, investing approximately $164 million in K–12 education in 2013, most of it to charter schools. Their core strategy as philanthropists, they say, is to infuse competitive pressure into America's K–12 education system.[51] Why? Who benefits?

Microsoft has invented its own elaborate system of controlled foreign corporations to reduce the amount of taxes it pays by billions of dollars each year (estimated at $2.43 billion in 2011, by a Senate investigation).[52] The Gates Foundation has spent billions of dollars since 2008 to accumulate long-term decision-making power and reshape the "playbook" for federal education policy according to Gates's whims, most of which have more to do with managerial intuition and deregulation than with research.[53] Most visibly, the failure of the small schools movement can be laid at the feet of the Gates Foundation. As education reporter Joanne Barkan has observed, the appointment of Arne Duncan as the US Secretary of Education was a coup for corporate reformers, but especially for Gates, with Duncan's first chief of staff coming straight from the foundation.

By entering into philanthropic partnerships with schools and installing their well-intentioned employees in classrooms

---

51   "K–12 Education," waltonfamilyfoundation.org.
52   Walter Hickey, "It's Not Just Apple: The Ultra-Complicated Tax Measures That Microsoft Uses to Avoid $2.4 Billion in U.S. Taxes," *Business Insider*, May 21, 2013, businessinsider.com.
53   Joanne Barkan, "Got Dough? How Billionaires Rule Our Schools," *Dissent*, Winter 2011, dissentmagazine.org.

to "develop talent," businesses are able to optimize the way their funds are used for their benefit, putting themselves— rather than parents, students, or teachers—in the position of defining what constitutes a good education. The ambition for what has come to be called social, venture, or strategic philanthropy is creating value, which is done by selectively choosing grantees and obligating them to meet the philanthropist or "investor's" performance goals. The movement's refrain, "Companies do well by doing good," shows who is reaping the rewards.[54]

US corporations and the Department of Education are actively pushing for a public education that includes greater exposure to STEM fields as a way to secure health and prosperity for the nation. In November 2014, President Obama became the first president to write a line of code during the Hour of Code, an online event to promote Computer Science Education week, whose corporate partners include Amazon, Apple, Best Buy, College Board, Facebook, Google, Khan Academy, Microsoft, LinkedIn, and Target. The event was followed by commitments from more than sixty school districts across the country to offer computer science classes to students. This is presumed to be a mutually beneficial arrangement, when in fact it serves only to benefit the interests of business. But, as David Berliner and Gene V. Glass, senior researcher at the

---

54   Michael E. Porter and Mark R. Kramer, "Philanthropy's New Agenda: Creating Value," *Harvard Business Review*, November–December 1999, hbr.org; and John Kania, Mark Kramer, and Patty Russell, "Strategic Philanthropy for a Complex World," *Stanford Social Innovation Review* 12, no. 3 (Summer 2014), ssireview.org.

National Education Policy Center, have pointed out, not only is our nation not experiencing a shortage of college graduates in STEM fields, but a number of those with degrees in STEM fields face unemployment. A 2004 government-sponsored report referenced by Berliner and Glass found,

> Despite recurring concerns about potential shortages of STEM personnel in the U.S. workforce, particularly in engineering and information technology, we did not find evidence that such shortages have existed at least since 1990, nor that they are on the horizon.[55]

The projected increase from 2012–22 in the need for personal care aides, a job requiring less than a high school diploma, dwarfs both the percentage increase and increase in number of jobs in STEM-related work such as information security and market research analysts, genetic counselors, audiologists, dental hygienists, and even nurse practitioners.[56] The jobs of the future will much more likely involve latex gloves and hair nets than white lab coats; today's students are far more likely to need to know how to care than how to code.

Still, corporate education "reformers" continue to push

---

55   David C. Berliner and Gene V. Glass, *50 Myths and Lies That Threaten America's Public Schools: The Real Crisis in Education* (New York: Teachers College Press, 2014).

56   "Table 4. Fastest Growing Occupations, 2012 and Projected 2022," United States Department of Labor, Bureau of Labor Statistics, December 19, 2013, bls.gov.

for the adoption of scientific management strategies in class-rooms across the country, particularly those in urban districts, aiming to bring to life liberal ideals of equal opportunity for *all children*, with well-documented disastrous results for *poor children*. These include the implementation of annual high-stakes assessments linked to state standards, which must be taken by all students regardless of ability (students with special needs take the same tests as every other child, and the only accommodation is that they are asked to sit for *double* the time as other students); requirements that states sanction and ultimately close "failing" public schools, which in practice turn out nearly without exception to be schools serving low-income students; as well as the use of value-added measurements, a discredited statistical measure that attempts to determine teacher quality based on student outcomes on standardized tests, to evaluate teachers. A 2013 report on the Obama administration's Race to the Top program—in which states competed for funds by implementing this package of "reforms"—found that implementation may actually be widening "opportunity gaps" rather than narrowing them.[57]

Even if we concede the idea that education should be preparation for one's role in the labor force, training the majority of the nation's children in computer science and engineering when there are already more qualified workers in

---

57   Elaine Weiss, *Mismatches in Race to the Top Limit Educational Improvement: Lack of Time, Resources, and Tools to Address Opportunity Gaps Puts Lofty State Goals Out of Reach* (Washington, DC: Broader, Bolder Approach to Education, September 12, 2013), boldapproach.org.

those industries than there are jobs in them does not serve the needs of children, but those of businesses—by increasing competition and cheapening what they will pay for qualified laborers.

3
EDUTOPIA: AGAINST TECHNICAL FIXES TO POLITICAL PROBLEMS

A year ago, at professional development training, I was asked to imagine what kind of school I would design if I had $5 million. I scribbled down a few ideas and shared them with the group. Most of us wrote things like "SMALLER CLASSES! A BIGGER BUILDING! WORKSHOPS AND SERVICES FOR PARENTS!" Even "INTERNET ACCESS IN THE CLASSROOM!" Then, we were asked to consider how we might implement changes to address the problems without the money. We talked about using space efficiently, installing shelving on the walls, and the intent to stay organized and prepared even though there are never enough hours in the day.

The point, in retrospect, is this: Forget that time is limited. Forget cash, or the lack of it, and that American teachers spend a collective $1.6 billion dollars a year—half of the $3.2 billion spent in total—supplying their classrooms with materials.[1] *You can do anything you put your mind to.* But can you?

---

1   The data is from a 2013 retail market study conducted by the National

Can we, teachers and administrators, create utopian learning environments through sheer force of will and innovation? Can we think our way out of inequality?

Neoliberal scholars[2] and politicos who seized upon *A Nation at Risk* during the late 1980s and early 90s to argue that American schools were globally uncompetitive and in need of a lifesaving injection of free-market principles succeeded in turning a controversial, unsubstantiated proposition into conventional wisdom almost overnight. Today many political officials, along with nearly every corporate philanthropist, take it for granted that a lack of accountability and rigor has left the education system in a state of *crisis*. This belief has, in turn, paved the way for those who are "socially conscious" but apolitical (for example, the rising figure of the "social entrepreneur"[3]) to frame education and poverty as

---

School Supply and Equipment Association (NSSEA), not from an advocacy organization. According to the study, 99.5 percent of all public school teachers spend some of their own money on school supplies, instructional materials, and other classroom materials. On average, the teachers surveyed reported spending $268 on school supplies, $491 on instructional materials, and $186 on classroom supplies ($945 total per teacher) that school year. The Education Market Association, *Retail Market Awareness Report, 2013 Edition*, edmarket.org.

2   The Hoover Institution employs many of these scholars, including Paul Hill, Michael J. Petrilli, and Eric Hanushek. Petrilli and Hanushek appear throughout this book. The distinction between scholar of education "reform" and political advisor is not hard-cut, as scholars often end up in government, and government officials end up at think tanks—one example is Terry Moe, who wrote the playbook on this kind of reform, as discussed in the previous chapter.

3   Or at least, *imagine* their actions could possibly be apolitical. For example, in 2012, *Forbes* magazine published a "30 Under 30: Social Entrepreneurs" (forbes.com) feature highlighting thirty startup organizations like the Global Poverty Project and the Future Project; the latter works "to help underserved kids reshape their schools and discover their passions" by placing "Dream Directors" in urban schools to encourage kids to "dream

bipartisan technical challenges in search of methodological solutions. Naturally, the solutions that spring from the minds of business school–trained advocates are rather more likely than those thought up by teachers or parents or students themselves to be based on the widespread adoption of a new technology or design or habit of mind, instead of something with as high an overhead as increasing or redistributing material resources.

In their book, *The Business Solution to Poverty: Designing Products and Services for Three Billion New Customers*, CEO Paul Polak and Mal Warwick argue that government efforts to address poverty "have not reached scale because they lack the incentives of the market to attract massive resources." One of the authors, Polak, a millionaire by way of oil and real estate, is the founder of two nonprofit organizations, International Development Enterprises and "design incubator" D-Rev, as well as a for-profit social venture called Windhorse International, whose mission is "inspiring and leading a revolution in how companies design, price, market, and distribute products to benefit the 2.7 billion customers who live on less than $2 a day." Warwick is a social venture capitalist. Together they outline design principles for the creation of new products and services based on "what [the poor] really want and need" plus "the ruthless pursuit of

---

up and build their own Future Projects." Projects kids have worked on include a documentary on bullying and a benefit fashion show to end leukemia. These organizations share two fundamental characteristics: reliance on business language ("governance") and networks, and the framing of issues as apolitical problems, decontextualized from history, that everyone has an equal stake in ending.

affordability." The book won a 2014 Axiom Business Book Award and received favorable reviews from the *Economist*; Rajiv J. Shah, administrator for the US Agency for International Development; former Obama administration official Van Jones; and from Bill Clinton, who called it original, ambitious, and practical—"one of the most hopeful propositions to come along in a long time."

"Harness[ing] the power of free enterprise," he wrote, may "be the key to reducing the number of people in poverty on a very large scale . . . while making a profit."[4] This is not a niche argument that appeals to a cult following, but a significant development covered regularly by *Forbes*, CNBC, *Harvard Business Review*, *Fast Company*, *Business Week*, and other denizens of the culture.[5] Capitalism has acquired (another) new spirit: for-profit social entrepreneurs aim to "do good while making money," and corporate philanthropists expect to get a "return on investment" and shape the strategy and goals of the nonprofit organizations to which they donate.

In a 2010 talk with Massachusetts Institute of Technology students, Bill Gates of Microsoft and the Bill and Melinda Gates Foundation—ranked as the richest man in the world for sixteen of the past twenty years[6]—asked, "Are the brightest minds working on the most important problems?"

---

4   "Testimonials," businesssolutiontopoverty.com.

5   Ankur Jain, "The Rise of the Young Social Entrepreneur," CNBC, November 19, 2014, cnbc.com; and Lara Galinsky, "Not Everyone Should be a Social Entrepreneur," *Harvard Business Review*, July 19, 2012, hbr.org.

6   Alexandra Sifferlin, "Bill Gates Is the Richest Man in the World (Again)," *Time*, March 3, 2014, time.com.

Gates's intention was to be provocative; following the assumption that "doing good" and doing business are harmonious and interrelated ends, he urged students who might otherwise go into investment banking or the tech industry to consider "global development" instead. In the same talk, he identified what he sees as the two most significant issues of our time: improving the lives of the world's poorest people and improving education, encouraging future research into the technology of open source learning platforms and what makes someone a good teacher. "I had no idea of how poorly the education system in the U.S. is working," he added. Gates "envisions a system that brings together the best lectures and course materials, and blends them with interactive elements and user feedback and possibly the opportunity for accreditation," reported MIT's student newspaper, the *Tech*.[7]

Whether or not Microsoft and Google will cop to it, every hope for and vision of the future is ideological, because *progress* is subjective: Imagining what it should look like and how we ought to get there requires us to make judgments about what is desirable and what is not. "Design thinking" is a phenomenon embraced by the business community to determine priorities and arrive at simple, creative resolutions to the problems it has identified. Its most prominent

7   Jeff Guo and Rob McQueen, "Gates Asks Students to Tackle World's Problems," *Tech*, April 23, 2010, tech.mit.edu. Ironically, at the same time that education is conceived of as a problem, it is also seen as a solution, specifically, to poverty: The School-in-a-Box, which contains pencils, scissors, counting cubes, and "culturally neutral" content like exercise books and posters of number tables and the alphabet, is now part of UNICEF's standard emergency response operations around the world: "School-in-a-Box," unicef.org.

evangelist, Tim Brown, CEO of global design company IDEO and a regular at Davos and TED talks, has described design thinking as a way to infuse "local, collaborative, participatory" planning into the development of products and organizational processes.[8] IDEO, which first became noteworthy for creating the Apple mouse, was recently hired to design an entire South American school system from the ground up.

The firm's mission to "create impact through design" encompasses consulting for private companies like health insurer Kaiser Permanente, as well as a nonprofit side—Brown sits on the board—that has partnered with the Bezos Family Foundation to campaign about the importance of engaged parenting and developed an online "educational experience" (funded in part by a $3 million grant from the Bill and Melinda Gates Foundation) that is now one of ten preferred institutions Walmart directs its workers to for higher education.[9] IDEO.org "practices human-centered design to solve some of the world's most difficult problems," says the organization's home page, and "works to empower the poor."

One of those problems is, perhaps not surprisingly, education. To that end, IDEO has published an 81-page "Design Toolkit" made available to teachers worldwide as a free download.[10] It contains no physical tools but features

---

8   "Tim Brown: Designers—Think Big!," TED Global 2009, ted.com.
9   Paul Fain, "Catholic College, Online Degrees," *Inside Higher Ed*, April 28, 2014, insidehighered.com.
10   ideo.com/work/toolkit-for-educators.

attractive blank graphic organizers, fun neon yellow text
boxes, and an array of vibrant photographs of groups of
people sitting in circles surrounded by hundreds of color-
coded Post-its. "Responsibility" is used three times in the
workbook, always in reference to teachers' role to generate
fixes and to develop what the firm calls "an evolved perspective," guided by a series of prompts. (The word "funding" is
used not at all—nor is the word "demand.")

Problems presented in floating speech bubbles range from
"I just can't get my students to pay attention" to "Students
come to school hungry and can't focus on work." All are
defined as "opportunities" for design in disguise. We're told
faculty at one school embarked on a "design journey,"
coming to an approach they call "Investigative Learning,"
which addresses students "not as receivers as information,
but as shapers or knowledge"—without further detail as to
how exactly this was accomplished.

Of course, the idea of engaging students as experienced
coteachers in their own education isn't novel, nor is it an
innovation brainstormed by a single group of teachers using
graphic organizers to chart solutions. It has a long history,
including Southern Freedom Schools and some of the educational projects taken up by the Black Panthers. Marxist educator Paulo Freire developed his critique of the traditional
"banking model" of education (in which students' minds are
regarded as passive vaults for teachers to toss facts into like
coins) in the 1960s and 70s, arguing that authentic education
is a task for radicals, not carried on "by A *for* B," but "by A
with B." His *Pedagogy of the Oppressed* helped reignite the

progressive education movement during that era, and his call for a meaningfully collaborative approach to learning remains influential in American schools of education today.

Peter McLaren, who taught elementary and middle school in a public housing complex for five years before becoming a professor of education, has since further developed Freire's ideas into an extensive body of revolutionary critical pedagogy, which encourages students to theorize about their own experiences and think about how they can fight against forms of exploitation, and which I was assigned in my first class as a master's student in education.[11]

Yet, here we are, a "nation at risk" with lower test scores than our international peers and children still arriving at school every day without eating breakfast. IDEO urges teachers be optimistic, to simply *"believe* the future will be better."

Like all modern managerial philosophies that stake their names on innovation, "design thinking" has not actually been put forward by theorists or implemented by business leadership because its ideas are new.

What design thinking ultimately offers is not evolution,

---

11 McLaren calls himself a humanist Marxist: "When the wet-sock formlessness of postmodern theory was becoming an unwitting companion of neoliberalism, I was mocked by some in the field for returning to a discredited Marxism. But the more our daily toil and struggle in the sloughs of ordinary human existence and human suffering increased, and the more our journey in the fearful paradoxicality of everyday life contrasted with the neat and seamless principles of the neoliberal logic of privatization, the more rational Marxism sounded to me. Critical pedagogy has a transnational heritage. There is no final resting place in the vault of the critical pedagogy pantheon, since critical pedagogy is constantly reinventing itself to meet the challenges of the present." "Critical Pedagogy against Capitalist Schooling: Towards a Socialist Alternative: An Interview with Peter McLaren," *Global Education Magazine*, April 7, 2013, globaleducationmagazine.com.

but the look and *feeling* of progress on the cheap, paired with the familiar, gratifying illusion of efficiency. It offers the illusion that structural and institutional problems can be solved through a series of cognitive actions—and finally, the suggestion that macro-level inputs (textbooks, teacher salaries) can remain the same, while outputs (test scores, customer service) improve. From the perspective of capitalism, this is magic, the only alchemy that matters.

Design Thinking for Educators urges teachers to be optimistic without specifying why, and to simply believe the future will be better. The toolkit instructs teachers to have an "abundance mentality," as if problem solving is a habit of mind. Why not "start with 'What if?' instead of 'What's wrong?'" they ask.

There are many reasons to start with "What's wrong?" That question is, after all, the basis of critical thought. Belief in a better future feels wonderful if you can swing it, but it is passive, irrelevant, inert without analysis about how to get there. The only people who benefit from the "build now, think later" strategy are those who are in power in the present.

It's not surprising, then, that when Carlos Rodríguez-Pastor Persivale,[12] the billionaire son of an elite Peruvian banking family, decided to expand his empire of restaurants

---

12 Rodríguez-Pastor Persivale's family fled Peru—where his father had been CEO of the Peruvian Central Bank—for California in 1968. He received his MBA from Dartmouth, established a hedge fund subsidiary of Santander in New York City, and purchased an Upper East Side penthouse for $27.5 million, suing upon discovering he was expected to share the terrace. He returned to Peru shortly thereafter.

and movie theaters by buying up a chain of for-profit English-language elementary schools, his first step was to contact IDEO and commission them to design everything: the buildings, the budget, the curriculum, professional development opportunities for teachers. The network is called Innova, and it's on its way to becoming the largest private school system in Peru.

According to "ed tech community" EdSurge, Innova is "more than just an example of how first-world ideas about blended learning and design thinking can be adapted in a developing country," aiming to close the achievement gap, build Peru's next generation of leaders, "and make a profit while doing so."[13]

Innova students use computer-tutoring programs designed by Pearson, the largest education company in the world, and Sal Khan, a protégé of the Gates Foundation. (By now, Khan's story is canonical among readers of the *Harvard Business Review*: In 2005, the former hedge fund analyst created a simple computer program for practicing math problems and some instructional videos to help tutor his cousins remotely. These went viral on YouTube among families looking for enrichment activities for their children at the end of the school day, one of which was Bill Gates's.) In a photograph of one location posted to IDEO's website, students sit in groups of six, each absorbed in his or her laptop. The school's modular walls collapse to allow classes of thirty to be

---

13 Christina Quattrocchi, "What a Peruvian School Designed by IDEO Looks Like," EdSurge, August 13, 2014, edsurge.com.

joined together into one large group of sixty students at various times throughout the day.

Khan said he was "blown away" after visiting: "It was beautiful, open, and modern. It was inspiring to see an affordable school deliver an education that would rival schools in the richest countries." The question is, affordable for whom?

Tuition at an Innova school is $130 a month, which is certainly considerably less than the cost of your average American private school but would require shelling out over a quarter of the monthly income of a family living on Peru's median household income of $430 a month. Half of the families that attend Innova are led by two parents working professional jobs such as accounts, engineers, or entrepreneurs. For his part, Rodríguez-Pastor has been clear that the schools are targeted specifically at Peru's emerging middle class, but American education reformers have a different sense of what the schools represent.

IDEO interprets the fact that Innova students perform at higher than the national average on math and communication tests as proof that they've delivered on their mantra for the project, "affordability, scalability, excellence." But if test scores are higher than the public schools', it is not because of the soul-searching of teacher/designers. It's because tuition is about a quarter of the national median income. After all, a consistent pattern in educational research of the past half century is that the socioeconomic status of a child's parents is one of the strongest predictors of his or her academic success.

"Usually in Peru, our schools are like a jail," says Innova founder Jorge Yzusqui Chessman. "But [Innova] schools . . .

have big transparency, many colors, and bandwidth through-out." Transparency and Wi-Fi for the middle class, while everyone else attends schools "like jails"?

Given the data, perhaps it would be more revolutionary, more innovative, and more forward-thinking if, instead of free idea toolkits, IDEO built a system that ensured every child, rich and poor, had access to these beautiful new schools. There is one simple, elegant solution: Make them free and public, and tax rich business owners like Persivale to pay for them.

On the other hand, American historian of education Larry Cuban has observed that even when innovations *are* well funded for mass use in public schools—during the Baby Boom, for instance, over $100 million was invested by the federal government and the Ford Foundation to promote the use of televisions in classrooms as a strategy for the alleviation of a teacher shortage—they rarely change the fundamental nature of schooling.[14] When we think about the classrooms of the future, we have to ask what (as Marshall McLuhan has put it) technology like radio and television can do that the present classroom can't. That means asking, what's futuristic about the future? And equally importantly—to whom will it belong?

---

14 Larry Cuban, *Teachers and Machines: The Classroom Use of Technology Since 1920* (New York: Teachers College Press, 1986).

Teaching machines

Technology offers real possibilities for changing the way we relate to each other for the better—for example, adaptive technology for children with special needs gives us the potential to integrate children with even severe disabilities into general education classrooms. But there's a disconnect between what we imagine technology can do and what it truly will do, much like the divide between what we imagine education can do and what it actually does. One laptop per child can't lift communities out of poverty, because the entire global economy is structured to keep the wealthiest people—who have no interest in paying people more or making other concessions to workers, and indeed, are compelled by market competition to keep cutting costs—in power.

Management gurus and their tech-industry followers insist that if we can dream it, we can do it; that instead of "throwing more money at the problem," we must use our creativity to brainstorm *best practices* for education and make them *scalable*. Harvard Business School Professor Clayton Christensen believes that in the future, computer-based instruction will entirely replace the current model, bringing a higher return on investment for the nation's education system.

Today's corporate education reformers express frustration with the continuity of traditional schooling methods— though most do not recognize the history to which they are intimately tied, since technological innovation is imagined to be as ahistorical as it is apolitical. In a 2013 Google+ hangout,

US Secretary of Education Arne Duncan told Silicon Valley–based social entrepreneur Sal Khan:

> We have to continue to accelerate. The fact that we're still teaching with a nineteenth-century model makes no sense whatsoever, with twenty-five or thirty kids sitting in rows learning the same thing at the same time, same pace. It's like Neanderthal. It makes no sense. This idea with technology being a great thing to empower moving from seat time to competency—I don't want to know how long you sat there, I want to know, do you know the materials? Do you know algebra or biology or chemistry or physics? If you know it, you shouldn't have to sit there.[15]

Edward Thorndike, the behavioral psychologist known for introducing scientific methods into the field of education, shared this frustration when he first theorized the possibility of a teaching machine. Textbooks, he observed in 1912, prod a student toward reasoning but are unable to manage the process of elucidating just enough to help a student arrive at his or her own conclusions.[16]

Described by colleagues as prodigious, efficient, and "an extremely rapid reader" who preferred to read books in one sitting, smoking cigarettes between chapters, Thorndike was preoccupied throughout his career with the quantification of

---

15   Roger Riddell, "Arne Duncan and Sal Khan Talk U.S. Education in Google+ Hangout," *Education Dive*, August 23, 2013, educationdive.com.
16   Ludy T. Benjamin Jr., "A History of Teaching Machines," *American Psychologist* 43, no. 9 (September 1988): 703–12, aubreydaniels.com.

human intelligence—he would go on to create an aptitude test used by the American military during World War I, as well as college entrance exams—but his objection to the use of textbooks in classrooms is an argument against standardization, or at least against learning at a single standard pace mediated by a teacher.[17]

Thorndike envisioned a future in which texts were capable of offering a self-directed learning experience for school children: If, "by a miracle of mechanical ingenuity," he wrote, a book could be arranged to hide information and display it step-by-step, so that page 2 was only accessible upon mastery of page 1, "much that now requires personal instruction could be managed by print"—effectively making the teacher as guide obsolete.

Four decades later, B. F. Skinner, a man who believed in neither free will nor hope for the world's salvation, stood in front of a new kind of classroom and announced that the future was here.[18] Skinner had been influenced by the work of Sidney Pressey, a psychologist who, following Thorndike's research on the retention of information through practice, developed a machine he believed would generate an industrial revolution in education (Pressey himself was deterred by the Great Depression).[19]

---

17   Robert S. Woodworth, *Edward Lee Thorndike, 1874–1949: A Biographical Memoir* (Washington, DC: National Academy of Sciences, 1952).

18   Joel Greenberg, "B. F. Skinner Now Sees Little Hope for the World's Salvation," *New York Times*, September 15, 1981, nytimes.com.

19   Sara McNeil, "Sidney Pressey," *A Hypertext History of Instructional Design*, faculty.coe.uh.edu/smcneil.

"I am B. F. Skinner, professor of psychology at Harvard University. I should like to discuss some of the reasons why studying with a teaching machine is often dramatically effective," he announces in a video from 1954.[20] On screen, we see an enormous group of teenage children sitting elbow-to-elbow at long tables, rapidly and silently inputting answers into a device that looks like a cross between a typewriter and a record player. In the window of each child's machine is an incomplete sentence or an equation missing a piece. Once the student fills in the blanks, the machine confirms or corrects the answer. Every child works alone. Skinner reflects,

> The machine you have just seen in use . . . is a great improvement over the system in which papers are corrected by a teacher where the student must wait perhaps until another day to learn whether or not what he has written is right. Such immediate knowledge . . . most rapidly [leads] to the formation of correct behavior."

Skinner was not only concerned with increasing the efficiency of knowledge absorption for the individual learner, but also for the group. He leaves us with this:

> With techniques in which a whole class is forced to move forward together, the bright student wastes time waiting for others to catch up, and the slow student, who may not

---

20   "B. F. Skinner. Teaching Machine and Programmed Learning (1954)," posted by Giovanni Bonaiuti, December 20, 2011, youtube.com.

be inferior in any other respect, is forced to go too fast . . .
A student who is learning by machine moves at the rate
which is most effective for him.

For Skinner, as well as for corporate education "reformers," knowledge is static and students are passive recipients;
efficient transmission of information is the goal of education.
And technology is the means by which we make the transmission process faster, cheaper, smarter. Gifted children are best
served by moving individually at their own pace, "slow
students" move at theirs, in isolation. This way of conceptualizing learning corresponds neatly with our present
economic system, in which individuals either stand or fall on
their merits, but it fails to deal with—conceals, in fact —the
contentiousness of reality.

Skinner's new classroom went through many iterations
over the decades that followed—a more sophisticated version
known as Individually Prescribed Instruction (IPI) was used
by students at Pittsburgh's Oakleaf Elementary in 1965, and
described by a contemporary journal of education as "the
nation's first successful operation of individualized instruction on a systematic, step-by-step basis"—but his teaching
machine was never adopted on a mass scale in American
public schools.[21]

Part of the resistance to the technology came from educators. Newly professionalized, they were adamantly opposed

21   Larry Cuban, "The Past Lives on in the Present: Customized
Learning Then and Now," *Larry Cuban on School Reform and Classroom
Practice* (blog), January 19, 2013, larrycuban.wordpress.com.

to the transformation of their role to coordinator. Rodney Tillman, the dean of the George Washington University School of Education, wrote in an essay titled simply "Do Schools Need IPI? No!" that the functions of a teacher using the system are limited to "writing prescriptions for courses of study, diagnosing student difficulties, and tutoring . . . These I cannot accept."[22]

Tillman was not resistant to the use of technology in schools so much as he was hostile to the particular vision of learning implicit in teaching machines, which rewarded rote mastery while evaluating student performance in isolation. The skills required to prepare children for the future were, he argued, not didactic but interpersonal.

And even in neurotic post-Sputnik America, parents tended to share a belief in the broadly humanist model of education. In 1960, the National Education Association (NEA) found it necessary to release a statement reassuring concerned mothers that while mechanical aids were now part of a modern classroom, they would never be the mode of instruction. "NEA Allays Parent Fears on Robot Teacher" was the headline in the *Oakland Tribune*.[23]

Anxiety about technology in classrooms—or, robots raising the children—was crystallized in pop culture: *The Jetsons*, which premiered in 1962, is the story of a typical nuclear family in the year 2062. George Jetson works a few hours a week at

---

22   Rodney Tillman, "Do Schools Need IPI? No!" *Educational Leadership* 29, no. 6 (March 1972): 495–8.

23   Matt Novak, "The Jetsons Get Schooled: Robot Teachers in the 21st Century Classroom," *Smithsonian.com*, March 19, 2013, smithsonianmag. com.

Spacely's Sprockets, Jane Jetson is a homemaker, and young
Elroy Jetson's teacher is a robot named Ms. Brainmocker.

By 1981, at the end of his life, Skinner would recant his
belief that the technology could solve the world's problems,
observing bitterly that no one had had the inclination to use
the tools he'd created. Skinner was not alone in his desire to
radically transform education for a new century, or in his
eventual disillusionment with this project. Just a few decades
prior to the development of the teaching machine, Thomas
Edison had declared that books were obsolete and motion
pictures would initiate a revolution of the school system
within ten years—a process that is still dramatically incomplete over a hundred years later.

The possibilities of education technology remain ambigu-
ous. The tools with which we learn aren't intrinsically
empowering, as Skinner assumed and Arne Duncan continues to assume, or inherently threatening. They can be used in
ways that are liberating or oppressive. But the popular idea
that technological innovation is cruel ("Ms. Brainmocker") is
not irrational.

"Innovation" is almost always invoked by elites to elide
conflict over resources and class. Experts from Edison onward
called enthusiastically for the incorporation of film and radio
in classrooms without accounting for the fact that, as
historian David Tyack points out, there were still tens of
thousands of American schools that lacked electricity well
into the 1960s.[24] Of course, these schools were not evenly

---

24   David B. Tyack and Larry Cuban, *Tinkering Toward Utopia: A*

distributed across the country. They were the ones attended by rural and working-class children, particularly in communities of color.

American public schools are financed through a uniquely decentralized combination of local, state, and federal funds. Approximately 44 percent of school funding comes from local revenues and 47 percent from states—usually in the form of business and residential property taxes—and only about 7 to 10 percent from the federal government. (Prior to the Johnson administration, none came from federal funding.) Thus schools in high-income areas receive markedly higher levels of funds.

The optimism of billionaires

In 1966, an MIT professor lamented that it had been easier to put a man on the moon than to reform public schools.[25] Today, SpaceX CEO Elon Musk wants to replace the US space shuttle program and "blow up education" by turning it into a game and adding special effects.[26]

"Give kids a chance to fly," Duncan said to Sal Khan in their Google+ hangout. "Let them find their passion and they'll go to the moon with that." Why are two such disparate concepts as education and space travel so intricately

Century of Public School Reform (Cambridge, MA: Harvard University Press, 1995).

25 Cuban, *Teachers and Machines*.

26 Matthew Lynley, "Elon Musk on Starting Small, Blowing Up Education and Reaching the Stars in 3 Years (Video)," *VentureBeat*, September 15, 2011, venturebeat.com.

linked in our public discourse? Education and space are both
metonymy for the future. When today's children will grow
into tomorrow's adults, holding meetings in holodecks and
beaming themselves through the galaxy in maroon turtle-
necks, they will have replaced us. When science fiction
becomes reality, we will all be dead.

Unless we figure out a way to bring about the impossible.
From the perspective of the tech industry, education and
space travel are alike because they are problems in search of
rational, personalized twenty-first-century answers, like
those arrived at by design thinking. The expectation is that
these answers will obliterate material limitations, class struggle—history, past and present. Design thinking, embraced
by key figures in business and especially in the tech industry,
insists that educators adopt a perpetually optimistic attitude
because that is what it takes to believe everything will turn
out OK if we just work together to streamline our efforts.
That is what it takes to believe that the *best* idea is the one that
survives group discussion and is adopted. The rabid opti-
mism of the techno-utopian vernacular, with its metaphors
that no longer register as metaphors, obscures the market
imperatives behind the industry's vision for the future.

It's intended to. Conflating the future with unambiguous,
universal progress puts us all on equal footing. Participation as
a citizen in this framework consists of donating your dollar,
tweeting your support, wearing your wristband, vowing not to
be complacent. Critique of the solution only impedes the eventual discovery of the solution. And why make demands of
power if you yourself are also empowered? Empowerment, as

Duncan uses it, is a euphemism. Anger is empowering, frustration is empowering—critique is empowering. *Competence* is not empowering.

The fact is, education is not a design challenge with a technical solution. It is nothing like building a spaceship. It is a social and political project that the neoliberal imagination insists on trying to innovate out of existence.

It won't be successful. Why? The most significant challenges faced today in education are not natural obstacles to be overcome by increasing productivity—they are man-made struggles over how resources are allocated.

In a frequently cited policy report on academic performance and spending over the past forty years, Andrew J. Coulson of the Cato Institute concludes that dramatic increases in education funding have not resulted in improvements in student performance. "In virtually every other field," Coulson notes,

> productivity has risen over this period thanks to the adoption of countless technological advances—advances that, in many cases, would seem ideally suited to facilitating learning. And yet, surrounded by this torrent of progress, education has remained anchored to the riverbed, watching the rest of the world push past it.[27]

What Coulson and others who repeat this myth ignore is *who* specifically is left out of the tech world's ecstatic march

---

27   Andrew J. Coulson, *State Education Trends: Academic Performance and Spending over the Past 40 Years*, Policy Analysis No. 746 (Washington, DC: Cato Institute, 2014), cato.org.

toward progress, and how and why.

The United States is one of only a few Organisation for Economic Co-operation and Development (OECD) countries, along with Israel and Turkey, where schools that serve rich families have better resources and higher funding than schools that serve poor families. A 2010 OECD report noted: In sixteen OECD countries, more teachers are allocated to disadvantaged schools to reduce the student-teacher ratio, with the objective of moderating disadvantage. This is particularly the case in Belgium, Italy, Ireland, Spain, Estonia, Iceland, Portugal, Japan, the Netherlands, and Korea. Only in Turkey, Slovenia, Israel, and the United States are disadvantaged schools characterized by a higher student-teacher ratio.[28]

In 2013, Andreas Schleicher, who runs the OECD's international educational assessments, told the *New York Times*: "The bottom line is that the vast majority of OECD countries either invest equally into every student or disproportionately more into disadvantaged students. The US is one of the few countries doing the opposite."[29]

In a country where the top 20 percent of the population earns eight times as much as the bottom 20 percent, this inevitably leads to two distinct and parallel systems of education, one for the rich and one for the poor. It's not that "money doesn't matter," or that technology can be a substitute for it,

28   Organisation for Economic Co-operations and Development, "Equity and Quality in Education: Supporting Disadvantaged Students and Schools (OECD Publishing, 2012), oecd.org.
29   Eduardo Porter, "In Public Education, Edge Still Goes to Rich," November 5, 2013, nytimes.com.

but that children from working-class and poor families score lower on standardized test scores than their wealthy peers—and America has many more poor families than rich.

Today, over 20 percent of children in the United States live in poverty. More than 1 million students in America were homeless during the 2010–11 school year, according to the US Department of Education. Overall, the poverty rate for Americans has declined steadily throughout the 1960s and 70s, reaching a low of 11 percent in 1973 before beginning to rise again in the 1980s, a pattern consistent with the policy shift from Johnson's Great Society programs to Reagan's cuts to public services.[30] While the poverty rate for people over sixty-five years of age has fallen dramatically since the advent of social security, children continue to represent a disproportionate share of the poor.

The presently high levels of economic and racial segregation in the United States has been linked to negative educational conditions and outcomes by Gary Orfield and Chungmei Lee of the Harvard University Civil Rights Project, whose study of metro Boston "shows a strong relationship between segregation by race and poverty and teacher quality, test scores and dropout rates."[31]

---

30 "Poverty in the United States: Frequently Asked Questions," National Poverty Center, The University of Michigan Gerald R. Ford School of Public Policy, npc.umich.edu.

31 Gary Orfield and Chungmei Lee, *Why Segregation Matters: Poverty and Educational Inequality* (Cambridge, MA: Civil Rights Project, Harvard University, January 2005), civilrightsproject.ucla.edu.

The cynicism of managers

Sal Khan's Khan Academy, an online learning platform funded by generous grants from the Gates Foundation, is the miracle of mechanical ingenuity that Thorndike dreamed of a century ago. When I first logged on to Khan Academy, I was surprised to find that despite all the tech-industry backing, it is not attractive, simple, or intuitive. Users mouse over the Subjects bar and choose Math, Science, Economics and Finance, Arts and Humanities, Computing, Test Prep, or Partner Content. Clicking on a Math "mission" brings you to a page of basic exercises. In instructional videos, Khan is awkward, a one-time mathlete with a slight twang and the affected exuberance of someone who has been teased but ultimately rewarded for being himself.

The website is interactive in the most mechanistic sense of the word: It provides individual feedback. After ten correct answers, the user can move on to the next concept. Ten correct answers is applied uniformly throughout the site as a metric, though it's unclear why success in this metric indicates mastery, just as the 85 percent correct metric of the IPI system seemed to be arbitrarily selected in order to enable the teaching machine to function. Badges, which are meant to be incentives, are exactly the kind of thing an "unabashedly geeky" adult would think a kid might find interesting.

It is a cloud-based, portable version of Skinner's teaching machine. Its strength is that it is self-guided: Exercises allow repetition and provide students with immediate feedback as they practice. Memory performance improves with practice, and practice leads to automaticity, which frees up working memory and allows us to concentrate on comprehension. That's why it's impossible to gain complex insight into the abstract concepts of literature or algebra until we can read words and equations fluently. Passive practice does not actually improve our recall of information, and Thorndike, who saw the mind as a group of habits, was the first to identify the use of feedback as essential to successful learning.

But where's the revolution? Khan is quick to say his videos are not a replacement for teachers, a claim that seems disingenuous given that the mission of his project is to "provide a free world-class education for anyone, anywhere." Pedagogically, the videos are unambitious. Even with a paper textbook, a student can move at his or her own pace and receive feedback by checking answers at the back of the book. Why should a digitized version create a significantly different outcome?

Khan Academy is a fine way to practice math problems or learn a didactic skill. What it is not is innovative in pedagogy or design. As a system of education it is a failure. It degrades both student and teacher by de-emphasizing the importance of interpretation and critique in education, just like design thinking does.

One example of the importance of this kind of flexible and evolving practice—*especially* for children from low-income families—comes from Lisa Delpit, educator and author of *Other People's Children* (1995). In talks, Delpit uses an example she witnessed in a preschool in which a teacher handed out a tray of candy and instructed children to each take a piece and pass on the tray. Some of the children took multiple pieces, and there was not enough to go around. A teacher evaluating the children without interpreting the context (like a machine) would conclude that the children did not successfully complete the task and need more practice in sharing. In fact, after asking why the children took extra pieces, the (human) teacher found that they were simply engaging in a different kind of creative economy, saving up a couple of pieces to take home to siblings later.

I suspect the innovation Gates is investing in is not a technological one, but a managerial one. The only truly novel thing Sal Khan has done is produce a cheap and popular way to distribute basic lectures and exercises to a large number of people, who like them. It's possible that what Gates admires most about him is that one man can teach so many different subjects and ages ranging from kindergarten math to cell biology to financial markets. At the Aspen Ideas Festival, Gates praised Khan for moving "about 160 IQ points from the hedge fund category to the teaching-many-people-in-a-leveraged-way category." Look, he seems to be saying, at all the value that can be extracted from one employee!

In a November 2012 interview, Gates told Fareed Zakaria,

When you revolutionize education, you're taking the very mechanism of how people become smarter and do new things and you're priming the pump for so many incredible things. Over the next decade at all levels in all countries, that's going to change quite dramatically . . .

[Technology] will take that space at the current investment levels and allow us to do a far better job.[32]

Gates has also repeatedly called for austerity in public education, repeating the familiar argument in a blog entry at the *Huffington Post* that for thirty years we've been spending increasing amounts of money while performance by American children remains flat.[33] What we need to do, he says, is raise performance without spending more by changing the way it is spent. To that effect, Arne Duncan asked a room full of Silicon Valley entrepreneurs and investors last year, "Can we find ways to scale the amazing teachers we do have?" Systems that "scale" retain quality under an increased workload. Modifying teachers to scale would mean replacing them with robots or computers.[34]

Managers are incentivized to outsource redundant jobs and tasks, but in the past thirty years there's been a special focus on chipping away the security and esteem of teachers and the American school system. Certainly it's about money, as it always is, but the financial backing of the Gates Foundation is astronomical enough that the question is less about actual scarcity and more about how the funds will be spent.

---

32   *Fareed Zakaria GPS*, interview with Bill Gates, November 18, 2012, transcripts.cnn.com/transcripts.

33   Bill Gates, "Flip the Curve: Student Achievement vs. School Budgets," *The Blog* (blog), *Huffington Post*, March 1, 2011, huffingtonpost.com.

34   Christina Farr, "U.S. Education Secretary's Stern Challenge to Entrepreneurs: We Have So Far to Go," *VentureBeat*, May 1, 2013, venturebeat.com.

The firing and disciplining of teachers is also a specific choice driven by corporate logic. Though they are atomized as workers into separate classrooms and competing districts, teachers are, as the American labor scholar Beverly Silver puts it, strategically located in the social division of labor: If they don't go to work, no one can—or at least, no one with children to look after.[35] As caretakers, teachers are by definition important and trusted community figures, public care workers who can shut down private production.

American teachers, and specifically, teachers' unions, have a complicated political past within the communities they teach. NYC's United Federation of Teachers (UFT), for example, supported a racist provision opposed by Black educators and community leaders including Martin Luther King Jr., which would have given teachers the power to expel "disruptive children" from their classrooms into separate schools. On the other hand, the radical Communist-backed Teachers Union that preceded the UFT was a strong and effective advocate for Black and Latino students during the Civil Rights Movement, pioneering "social movement" unionism.[36]

When teachers organize and advocate for their own rights along with the rights of their students—which are not opposed but palpably intertwined, since they are the two groups of people most affected on a daily basis—instead of

35 Beverly J. Silver, *Forces of Labor: Workers' Movements and Globalization Since 1870* (Cambridge, UK: Cambridge University Press, 2003).
36 Clarence Taylor, *Reds at the Blackboard: Communism, Civil Rights, and the New York City Teachers Union* (New York: Columbia University Press, 2011).

maintaining polite negotiations with business and the state or accepting their fate as passive widgets, the results are powerful. We see it in the work and ambitions of Chicago's Caucus of Rank and File Educators (CORE), the radical caucus comprised of dissident teachers working in collaboration with angry Chicago public school parents, which gained control of the Chicago Teachers Union (CTU) in 2012 and voted to strike, declaring open resistance to standardized testing and accountability as implemented by corporate reformers.[37] For four years, CORE had been meeting with parents and organizers to talk about how the teachers' fight against neoliberal reform could include and support the ongoing struggles against gentrification, overcrowding, school closings. "A pastor from the south-central neighborhood of Englewood named Rev. Hood focused his talk on the need to harness the power of the teachers' union to 'shut down the city,'" noted *Socialist Worker*.[38]

In the United States—where the vast majority of families continue to rate their own child's teacher highly, even while believing the political mantra that the nation's education system is rapidly deteriorating—unique job protections like tenure serve to further strengthen teachers' capacity to resist neoliberal reforms like budget cuts.

In the same vein, schools are public spaces in which children and teenagers can put down their pencils or laptops or

---

37 Micah Uetricht, "Strike for America: The CTU and the Democrats," *Jacobin* 9 (2012), jacobinmag.com.
38 "Building Teacher-Community Solidarity," SocialistWorker.org, September 2, 2008.

iPads and organize against state violence and coercion. A notable example is the student protests that took place around the country after the unarmed Black teenager Michael Brown was murdered by a police offer in Ferguson, Missouri, in 2014. Urban and suburban elementary schoolers, high schoolers, and college students from the Bronx to the Bay Area, where Brown's father stood with students in solidarity, to Evanston, Illinois, to Oakland, students organized "die-ins," rallies, walkouts, and marches, often with the full support of their teachers behind them.[39] Steve Singer, a teacher in Pittsburgh, wrote in the *Washington Post* about throwing out his lesson plan for the day and having a conversation with his students about racial injustice.[40] In Georgia, where teachers do not have collective bargaining rights (meaning no unions or tenure), a teacher was first threatened with a pay cut and then fired for joining her students in a walkout, even though she scheduled a substitute teacher to cover her class.[41] The possibilities for confronting injustice are so powerful that children (especially Black and brown children, but increasingly American children from all ethnic

39   Veronica Rocha, "Father of Michael Brown to 'Stand Strong' with Bay Area Teens," *Los Angeles Times*, December 15, 2014, latimes.com; Stephanie Kelly, "Evanston Township High School Students Protest Brown, Garner Decisions," *Daily Northwestern*, December 16, 2014, dailynorthwestern.com; Wesley Lowery, "At Ferguson High School, Everyone Has a Michael Brown Story," *Chicago Tribune*, November 20, 2014, chicagotribune.com; "Students Stage 'Die-in' Protest," News12 Bronx, December 12, 2014, bronx.news12.com.
40   Valerie Strauss, "In One Classroom, a Teacher Makes Michael Brown the Lesson of the Day," *Washington Post*, November 27, 2014, washingtonpost.com.
41   Zaid Jilani, "Georgia Teacher Fired for Protesting Michael Brown Decision," AlterNet, December 6, 2014, alternet.org.

and class backgrounds except the very wealthiest, who attend private schools) are literally policed and considered suspects in their own school buildings.

Teachers who encourage resistance to exploitation can be essential sources of reinforcement and guidance for kids. People do not learn to think critically and construct meaning in isolation—which is the assumption behind the trend for textbooks that respond individually to each student and allow them to move at their own pace. People argue, discuss, play, experiment, and converse. And, as Delpit writes:

> Only those who are authentically and critically literate can become the independently thinking citizens required for any society's evolution. The opportunity to achieve such levels of literacy is even more critical for those whom the larger society stigmatizes . . . When people of color are taught to accept uncritically texts and histories that reinforce their marginalized position in society, they easily learn never to question their position.[42]

Learning as a group is not a painless process. A "good" teacher knows her students well, respects them and earns their respect in return, and challenges them to aim for the highest reaches of what Soviet psychologist Lev Vygotsky called "the zone of proximal development"—their potential.

---

42 Lisa Delpit, *"Multiplication Is for White People": Raising Expectations for Other People's Children* (New York: New Press, 2012).

Katherine McKittrick, a professor of gender studies and author of *Demonic Grounds: Black Women and the Cartographies of Struggle*, has pointed out in response to the idea of "trigger warnings" being placed on college syllabi: The classroom isn't safe. It *should not* be safe. Teaching, says McKittrick, is a "day-to-day skirmish," and teachers must work hard to create classroom conversations "that work out how knowledge is linked to an ongoing struggle to end violence," to engage with the history that students bring with them into the classroom and challenge engrained assumptions.[43]

This winter, during the tech-industry-sponsored and US Department of Education–supported Hour of Code, Susan DuFresne, a kindergarten teacher and former teachers' aid with forty years of experience told me, "Children are not standard. They need unstructured play indoors and out to develop skills" like sharing, listening, cooperation, and self-regulation. The Hour of Code is a publicity stunt in which public school children from preschool up are given laptops and taught to code. DuFresne was vocally opposed: Kids "have different learning styles," she said. "Some learn faster with technology. But now children as early as third grade will be required to type written answers into textboxes, click and drag, and use multiple tech software tools on the Common Core tests." Still, her resistance had little to do with fear of new tools, and everything to do with the conceptualization of the role of technology in the classroom.

---

43   "Katherine McKittrick, Author of *Demonic Grounds*, on Trigger Warnings," *Bully Bloggers* (blog), December 17, 2014, bullybloggers.wordpress.com.

Another high school teacher, Brooke Carey, who has been working for over a decade in the NYC school system, agreed that technology is often used in public schools' classrooms in "a fairly traditional way," with iPads serving as a fancier version of pen and paper and smartboards functioning as computerized chalkboards or dry erase boards. In American public schools, teaching tools have been digitized and optimized for efficiency, but the content and philosophy remains the same.

Even Google engineers know this. An article in the *New York Times* reported on the popularity of the Waldorf model of education in Silicon Valley as if it were a contradiction: "A Silicon Valley School That Doesn't Compute." Waldorf incorporates creative and tactile experiences and tools including hammers and nails, knives, knitting needles, and mud—but not computers—into the curriculum. Engagement comes from the connection between children and their teachers, who stress critical thinking and aim to create interesting, inquiry-based lesson plans.

According to the *Times*, employees at Google, Apple, Yahoo, Hewlett-Packard, and even the chief technology officer of eBay send their children to the Waldorf School of the Peninsula. "The idea that an app on an iPad can better teach my kids to read or do arithmetic, that's ridiculous," Alan Eagle, a Google communications executive who's written speeches for Eric Schmidt, told the *Times*.[44]

---

44   Matt Richtel, "A Silicon Valley School That Doesn't Compute," *New York Times*, October 22, 2011, nytimes.com.

The great irony is that the very Silicon Valley reformers promoting and funding techno-utopian models for American school children refuse to submit their *own* children to anything like it, choosing more innovative pedagogical models instead of newer touch screens.

The classroom of the future

One of the most powerful moments for me as a beginning teacher was seeing a video of a lesson I gave. The recording enabled me to transcend biology: to get out of my own head and see myself as my students did, to notice and interpret rustlings and undercurrents that would have otherwise escaped me entirely due to purely physical limitations.

In an hour, I learned more about my practice than I had during months of supervisor evaluations. iPads are more than glorified expensive dry erase boards. They could be used, for example, to connect teachers, traditionally operating within the confines of their own individual classrooms, to each other for professional development and growth purposes: Why not film the lessons of experienced teachers and compile a national or global library of what an engaging lesson looks like, which would be immediately accessible to new teachers?

What the current conversation about designing the classrooms of the twenty-first century misses is that innovations do not take place outside of the political economy. What we call technology and the world we create with it is determined by the social and political landscape in which we are living today; all that we deem necessary, all that we wish would continue and all that we determine should end. Science and technology are human creations, and as such, they are not entirely objective, but open to and shaped by interpretation.[45]

For corporate education reformers, the animating purpose of technology in classrooms is to more efficiently develop human capital, to make some people smarter, faster, and sort out the rest into the discard pile of American capitalism: low-wage labor. Because industrial capitalism makes us all, workers and capitalists alike, dependent on the market for acquisition of the basic necessities of life, we live lives dominated by market imperatives.

The American education system is shaped by those market imperatives—at least for children in public schools. The rich know that JavaScript can be learned in a couple of weeks or months. Education for "empowerment" requires the time-consuming cultivation of a complex understanding of history and one's place in it, as well as how it continues to shape our relationships and political economy.

When we imagine successful teaching as instruction of X number of people achieving X level of fluency, we redefine it—whether done by human or machine—from a social (and potentially political) to a technical act.

Teachers must continue to be able to help children think critically about the ways that reality is reshaped by

---

45   As Marcuse wrote in *One-Dimensional Man*, "There is no such thing as a purely rational scientific order. The process of technological rationality is a political process" (Herbert Marcuse, *One-Dimensional Man* [London: Routledge, 2002], 172).

technology and changes in the mode of production. How will children who take Google for granted understand research and inquiry? What will friendship be like for "children of the electric age," who have the option of never losing contact with childhood friends thanks to Facebook? Who wins and who loses by the adoption of specific technologies?

It's impossible to say today how we should teach and learn about tomorrow's social relationships. We know they will be mediated by technology, but how? The particulars will be shaped by time and practice. But just to imagine the evolution of education in this way is to ask radical questions, beginning with the forbidden one, "What's wrong with education today?" That question is inextricably linked with, and leads to, an even bigger and more dangerous one: What's wrong with society?

In 1922, a journalist described the way technology changes our relationship to the world:

> To the schoolboy of the year 1995 history will not merely be something to be memorized out of books. It will be visualized and made real for him by the moving pictures that are being made now. The people of our time will not be mere history book ghosts to this boy but living creatures who smile at him and walk and play and love and hate and work and eat.[46]

---

46 Matt Novak, "Moving Pictures to Show Schoolboys of 1995 Our Time (1920)," *Paleofuture* (blog), November 21, 2008, paleofuture.gizmodo.com.

But this isn't the way we see history today. Today, we see history as a dying field, in a separate sphere from STEM education, its practitioners likened to the last speakers of a lost language bent on preserving it, and devalued by the paltry sums they're paid. Humanism is regarded as inherently opposed to machines. And yet, as our journalist of 1920 alludes, technology offers us the ability to form connections and experience intimacy with more people, dead and alive, and across time and space.

In a bestselling contemporary novel about Victorian England, the British novelist Sarah Waters has her protagonist notice that the most interesting thing about radio as an invention was not the initial shock of hearing voices across space—somehow, "it was even more uncanny to take the ear-phones off and realize that the whisper was still going on—to think that it would go on, as passionate as ever, whether one listened in to it or not."[47]

Over time, technology has transformed the way we relate to each other and the epistemological foundations of society—the way we perceive reality collectively. This is a truly radical opening for anyone who wants to change education, inside the classroom and outside of it. The question is: What will we do with it?

---

47 Sarah Waters, *The Paying Guests* (New York: Riverhead, 2014).

4
EVERY CHILD SHOULD HAVE 100 PARENTS: AGAINST PERSONAL FIXES TO POLITICAL PROBLEMS

Child development in the age of austerity

Teaching, like motherhood, is at once idealized as a sacrificial act and devalued because it comes from the heart. These are not only jobs but identities, aspects of what teacher and feminist thinker Silvia Federici refers to as "the female role that capitalism has invented for us."[1] The top occupations for American women are almost entirely in "care work."[2] For

---

1 Silvia Federici, *Wages against Housework* (Power of Women Collective and Falling Wall Press, 1975), caringlabor.wordpress.com. Federici was a co-organizer of the radical Wages for Housework social movement, which called for economic compensation for domestic labor as a way to draw attention to its value.
2 "Care work" comprises a diverse group of occupations; some of the most common are secretaries, elementary and middle school teachers, child care workers, teacher assistants, cashiers, nurses and health aids, waitresses, and customer service representatives.

example, nursing is 91 percent female and social work is 80.8 percent female nationally, while 95 percent of domestic workers nationally are female.[3] Elementary and middle school teachers are 81.8 percent female.

Given their nearly always close proximity to the young, female caretakers are seen as essential to engendering socially acceptable values in the next generation. This is a task so critical to the maintenance of social life that those who are entrusted with it are expected to undertake it out of sheer joy with no eye to monetary "rewards"—and so vital to the perpetuation of economic life that failure is unacceptable. Thus, unlike accountants or athletes or janitors, "negligent" mothers and "unqualified" teachers[4] are judged as *bad people*.

Women are, of course, still uniquely and primarily called upon in their capacity for physical reproduction—a capacity that can only be called a burden in a society where health care is neither universal nor free. They also bear the primary responsibility for ensuring that children are properly socialized, protecting society's ability to replicate itself not only biologically by culturally.[5] Thus the failure of teachers is

---

3   Linda Burnham and Nik Theodore, *Home Economics: The Invisible and Unregulated World of Domestic Work* (New York: National Domestic Workers Alliance, 2012), domesticworkers.org.

4   The question we must be asking is: By whose standards?

5   Seventy-six percent of K–12 teachers and 98 percent of preschool teachers are women, even while they continue to be underrepresented in education leadership roles. Teachers in training spend thousands of dollars on certification tests and master's degrees, usually subsidized entirely by the individual teacher and increasingly becoming requisite at the beginning of one's career. This is true of early childhood teachers, who can expect to make between $30,000 and $45,000 in New York City as head teachers, and

like the failure of mothers—unthinkable, *monstrous*, disgusting, the final antisocial act that threatens not only the fabric of the political economy but its perpetuation. The word "cure" comes from the Latin root *cura*, meaning "care."

I say "women," not simply "mothers," because motherliness is, in the words of Elizabeth Peabody, the founder of the first English-language American kindergarten, not confined to mothers of the body. Women who are not involved in child rearing in some way have long been defined by what they lack, "sad cases in this wicked world." (In one conversation I had with a concerned father, he tried to relate to me with, "You're a mother—you understand." I am not a mother, nor was there any reason for him to make that assumption other than that I spend my days caring for children, but *I did understand*.) For Peabody, writing in the mid-nineteenth century, the teaching of young children was "the perfect development of womanliness," a way for women who were not biological mothers to assume a "useful, natural" role in society that was still sufficiently sacred. What does it mean to work at the feet of God? To labor "outside" the economy?

Very little compensation, as it turns out. Peabody and other middle-class women constructed teaching as "women's work" in an attempt to bridge the properly feminine—emotional, spiritual—domain of the family with the masculine world of commodity production.[6] Domestic caretaking

---

for K–12 public school teachers, who make $43,530 according to the NYC Department of Education.

6 In this chapter, I discuss teaching and motherhood as feminized and naturalized roles; these are social constructs, not biological mandates—men can of course serve as teachers and (more arguably) "maternal" figures.

was recognized as either slavery or deserving a paycheck when performed for other people's children, but white women's engagement with the material world was acceptable only as long as teaching remained a calling from on high, explicitly (in Peabody's words) not to be regarded as a "business, but as a religion."

As it happened, this fit perfectly with the needs of local school boards. Between 1870 and 1921, the percentage of male teachers decreased from 41 to 16 percent.[7] At the same time men were walking away from the agrarian rhythms of the teaching profession to pursue higher-paying industrial jobs, a growing support for compulsory education dramatically *increased* the demand for teachers. Rather than increase wages for men's teaching positions to be competitive with manufacturing and management work, local school boards opted to recruit women instead, arguing that they were naturally better suited to the moral education of children.

Eager for an autonomous role that was compatible with the romantic ideology of separate spheres, many middle- and upper-class women were happy to comply by signing up for work as kindergarten teachers. K–12 public education was rapidly taken over by working-class women "who became the 'hands' in the new urban factories."[8] The development

---

7   Shaun P. Johnson, "The Status of Male Teachers in Public Education Today," *Center for Evaluation and Education Policy Brief* 6, no. 4 (Winter 2008); and Janet Guildford, "'Separate Spheres': The Feminization of Public School Teaching in Nova Scotia, 1838–1880," *Acadiensis* 22, no. 1 (Autumn 1992): 44–64, journals.hil.unb.ca.

8   Barbara Beatty, *Preschool Education in America: The Culture of Young Children from the Colonial Era to the Present* (New Haven, CT: Yale University Press, 1995).

of the teaching force in the twentieth century is not the story of a glass ceiling that had to be shattered, but the story of invisible glass walls propping up an entire economy.

Women have subsidized the development of a professional teaching and child-care labor force in the United States. The pay gap between teaching and other jobs requiring the same skills and credentials persists today. As of 2011, the median annual salary of a child-care worker was less than that of a parking lot attendant or janitor,[9] yet child-care workers are expected by employers to pay for expensive certification exams and to have advanced education. For example, in New York City, the Department of Health expects assistant teachers to have at least an associate's degree with a study plan toward a bachelor's, or a bachelor's degree with a study plan toward a master's degree for head teachers.

And despite the opening of fields to women besides the caring professions, teaching draws more women, not less, every year. In 1980, 67 percent of teachers were female. During the 2011–12 school year, over 76 percent were. Since the 1980s, both the number of women entering teaching and the proportion of teachers who are women has risen, while school administration remains overwhelmingly male.[10]

---

9   Brad Plumer, "Five Shocking Facts about Child Care in the United States," *Wonkblog* (blog), *Washington Post*, April 15, 2013, washingtonpost. com.
10   At the same time, the number of people of color who are teachers has been increasing, from 12.4 percent in 1987 to 17.3 percent of teachers in 2011–12. According to data from the Consortium for Policy Research in Education, "Growth in minority teachers outpaced growth in minority students and was over twice the growth rate of white teachers." Teachers of color are two to three times more likely than white teachers in urban schools

Teaching, with its "summers off" and workdays that sync with children's schedules, continues to function as a way for mothers to negotiate the conflicting demands of public and private life, offering more flexibility than other jobs to "balance" caretaking of one's own children with waged work.

The premise of 2012's notable book *The End of Men*[11]—a concept nearly as fatuous as the end of history—is that women have won the gender war, outperforming men in educational attainment and outpacing them as the majority of the waged-labor force for the first time in history. The economics of the new era may simply be better suited to women, observes author and *Atlantic* editor Hanna Rosin.[12] Certainly they are, and that is the point. What has been our prize? Women make less money than men even in traditionally "female-dominated" jobs like teaching, as the *New York Times* reported in 2013, and are overrepresented in fields that pay minimum wage.[13] As a report by the National Domestic Workers Alliance puts it, "Domestic workers are women doing women's work. Their paychecks bear witness to this

serving high numbers of students of color from low-income backgrounds, the target of most neoliberal education reforms. It is obvious who the agents and who the subjects are in corporate education reform. Richard Ingersoll and Henry May, "Recruitment, Retention and the Minority Teacher Shortage (Consortium for Policy Research in Education, 2011)," repository. upenn.edu.

11   Hanna Rosin, *The End of Men: And the Rise of Women* (New York: Riverhead, 2012).

12   Hanna Rosin, "The End of Men," *Atlantic*, July/August 2010, theatlantic.com.

13   Shaila Dewan and Robert Gebeloff, "More Men Enter Fields Dominated by Women," *New York Times*, May 20, 2012, nytimes.com.

simple truth."[14] This is not because we "lower our own expectations of what we can achieve," as *Lean In* author Sheryl Sandberg would have it.[15] In fact, as Bryce Covert, economic policy editor for *ThinkProgress* has noted, research shows that today's female MBAs advocate equally for increased compensation and promotions throughout their careers, but bosses still give men raises two and a half times larger.[16] Women can lean in all they want, but the hyper-exploitation won't end until managers and policy makers stop pressing down and extracting all they can.

A more salient discrepancy for the majority of women is the disproportionate effects of declines in social spending, since women on average have significantly higher health care expenditures than men, are twice as likely as men to receive food stamps and comprise about 85 percent of those receiving public assistance in the form of Temporary Assistance for Needy Families benefits.[17] More subtly, women are frequently relied upon in the workplace to provide service with a smile— the "people skills," like "social intelligence, open communication, the ability to sit still and focus,"[18] that are so desirable

---

14 Burnham and Theodore, *Home Economics*.

15 This is Sheryl Sandberg's argument in *Lean In: Women, Work, and the Will to Lead* (New York: Knopf, 2013).

16 Bryce Covert, "Yes, Virginia, There Is a Gender Wage Gap," *Nation*, August 15, 2012, thenation.com.

17 G. M. Owens, "Gender Differences in Health Care Expenditures, Resource Utilization, and Quality of Care," *Journal of Managed Care Pharmacy* 14, no. 3 Supplement (April 2008): 2–6; Rich Morin, "The Politics and Demographics of Food Stamp Recipients," Pew Research Center, July 12, 2013, pewresearch.org; and "Characteristics and Financial Circumstances of TANF Recipients," Office of Family Assistance, August 8, 2012, acf.hhs. gov.

18 Rosin, "The End of Men."

in the new service economy—skills that are understood to be "not the province of men," as Rosin writes, but "seem to come easily to women."[19]

Now, in the face of an extraordinarily high child-poverty rate—with more than 1 million American students homeless—and massive budget cuts to social programs like Head Start, which provides early childhood education, health and nutrition services to low-income children, teachers are expected to solve the crisis of *A Nation at Risk* by closing the "achievement gaps" in performance between Black and white children and between children from low-income families and their wealthier peers. The restoration of a society in crisis to a healthy meritocracy has been depoliticized and placed on the shoulders of the care worker at school and at home. In communities where after-school programs, counselors, art and music teachers, and nurses have been eliminated, the staff "lucky" enough to hold onto their jobs must strain to become all of these things, or leave.

This was the assumption and tone behind *Vergara v. California*, the June 2014 ruling by the California state court to strike down teacher tenure laws, a contractual right originally put in place to protect academic freedom in education. Judge Rolf M. Treu (appointed by the far-right Governor Pete Wilson, a strong advocate for deregulation) declared the laws unconstitutional because incompetent teachers "substantially undermine" a child's education, violating students'

---

19   Rosin, *The End of Men*.

right to equal educational opportunity, and "shocking the conscience."[20]

Vergara v. California was filed by the parent group Students Matter, founded by Silicon Valley tech entrepreneur David Welch, with nine students as plaintiffs. Welch, who paid all legal bills for the case, has said that he first became interested in the issue of teacher tenure when a superintendent told him what he needed to improve the schools was "control over [his] workforce."[21] Of course, "command over the workforce" is not limited to issues of salary and scheduling—it is highly political.

Before the institutionalization of tenure, 250 New York City teachers were forced out of the profession for having been past or present members of the Communist Party or refusing to take loyalty oaths. Teachers have been dismissed from California public schools for questioning the authority of a principal to require teachers to police school sports events on weekends and evenings, participating in a peaceful political demonstration, and for being a woman over forty (the woman in question, Elizabeth Baldwin, was eventually able to keep her job because of a tenure hearing).[22]

To be clear, tenure does not mean that a teacher *can't be fired*. Tenure secures, for teachers who've undergone a

20   *Vergara v. California Tentative Decision*, June 10, 2014, studentsmatter.org.

21   Betsy Kulman, "What Happens When Students Sue Their Teachers?," Al Jazeera America, August 1, 2014, america.aljazeera.com.

22   Fred Glass, *A History of the California Federation of Teachers, 1919–1989* (San Francisco: California Federation of Teachers at Warren's Waller Press, 1989).

probationary period of two to five years, due process, or the requirement that the state respects a person's legal rights even in firing decisions. It is a myth that thousands of incompetent and abusive teachers are sitting in rubber rooms triumphantly collecting their paychecks.

Like the racialized image of the welfare queen, the rubber-roomed teacher is an allegorical villain who feeds on taxpayer money and neglects her job to raise happy and healthy children, creating pathological delinquents. Society is robbed twice over, first of the money it takes to provide her with "unearned" income, and second of the productive human capital that might have been had the children stayed in school and been effectively educated.

During one visit to evaluate the preschool where I work, a NYC Department of Health consultant told me about her close friend, a teacher in Harlem with twenty-five years of teaching experience who was "rubber-roomed" when a new principal decided to fire her and hire two younger teachers with lower salaries in her place. The teacher was just a few years from retirement but so demoralized from waiting two years in a rubber room that she was debating on whether or not to quit, regardless of the effects on her pension. I don't know the teacher personally, but I know the story. It's an all-too-common one in urban education. New York City alone has 1,131 teachers in its Absent Teacher Reserve, many of whom lost their jobs when their schools were shuttered—and who, prior to 2005, would have been required to be hired before rookie teachers. Bloomberg ended that policy; now, "higher-paid ATRs say principals have snubbed in favor of rookies at starting salaries because teacher salaries come out of the school's budget," reports the *New York Post*.[23]

Key testimony in the tenure case was provided by Eric Hanushek, a Hoover Institution economist who claimed in an influential 1986 paper that there is no relationship between school expenditures and student performance.[24] Hanushek argues that every year a "grossly ineffective" teacher stays in the classroom reduces the future earnings of the class by thousands of dollars, "dramatically lowering the college chances and employment opportunities of students." These consequences in turn have an impact on national security—

The future economic well-being of the United States is entirely dependent on the skills of our population. Replacing the poorest performing 5 to 8 percent of teachers with an average teacher would, by my calculations, yield improved productivity and growth that amounts to trillions of dollars.[25]

His calculations rest entirely on the findings of value-added measures, which have been determined inadequate measures of teacher quality by the American Statistical Association. A month before *Vergara* went to trial, the

23   Susan Edelman, "City Tries to Cut Down Teachers without Permanent Jobs," *New York Post*, August 3, 2014, nypost.com.

24   Eric Hanushek, "The Economics of Schooling: Production and Efficiency in Public Schools," *Journal of Economic Literature* 24, no. 3: 1141–77, hanushek.stanford.edu.

25   Eric Hanushek, "Ending Tenure to More Easily Fire Bad Teachers Helps Everyone," *New York Times*, March 2, 2015, nytimes.com.

American Educational Research Association released the results of a study that definitively concluded that state value-added performance measures do not reflect the quality or content of teachers' instruction.[26]

Even more puzzling, two of the plaintiffs in the *Vergara* case attended charter schools, which do not offer teachers tenure, and two attended a pilot school where no tenure is awarded. Not one of the plaintiffs claimed to have had a "grossly ineffective" teacher.[27] Christine McLaughlin, a 2013 Pasadena teacher of the year who has been repeatedly recognized for excellence in teaching, was identified during the proceedings as a "very bad teacher" for not handing out a textbook or syllabus. (McLaughlin has publicly stated that neither of these things is true.) Neither the plaintiffs or Judge Treu, nor Hanushek or Welch ever defined what makes a teacher grossly ineffective. Instead, lawyers for the plaintiffs argued that ensuring due process in termination cases was too costly and time consuming for school districts.

Welch later commented to Al Jazeera, "What's happening to these children is a crime. And if it's really a crime, then it's got to be illegal." Perhaps, but who is the perpetrator? Teachers themselves? The public schools? Or the society

---

26 "Study: State Value-Added Performance Measures Do Not Reflect the Content or Quality of Teachers' Instruction," American Educational Research Association, May 13, 2014, aera.net; Andrew C. Porter and Morgan S. Polikoff, "Instructional Alignment as a Measure of Teaching Quality," *Educational Evaluation and Policy Analysis (EEPA)*, May 2014, epa.sagepub. com.

27 Diane Ravitch, "The Vergara Trial Teachers Were Not 'Grossly Ineffective,'" *Diane Ravitch's Blog*, June 11, 2014, dianeravitch.net.

that organizes them? As Pedro Noguera has observed, we don't blame doctors at Veterans Affairs hospitals for the unconscionable shortcomings of the VA system. Like teachers, doctors at VA hospitals are public-service sector workers in a public space that neoliberal policy makers would prefer to see privatized, so why don't doctors draw the same personal ire from reformers? Maybe it's because, unlike teaching, the practice of medicine has not been feminized.[28]

The fact is, research shows that *less than 30 percent* of students' academic achievement is even attributable to schools, and teachers do not control everything that goes on inside schools, including (for instance) building maintenance or discipline codes. A constant theme in interviews I conducted with New York City public school teachers from 2014 to 2015 was teachers' disagreement and resistance to what they saw as "stupid policies" that were disrespectful and unresponsive to the needs of students, such as the rule that requires teachers to police students wearing hats.

Hanushek himself calculated the effects of teacher quality as accounting for *only 7.5 percent of variation in student achievement*.[29] Outside-of-school factors carry *at least twice the weight* as school environments in predicting student achievement. Whether a child has significant early exposure to complex language from caregivers, access to medical care,

---

28 Nurses, on the other hand, experience similar working conditions as teachers, including neoliberal pressures by administrators to increase productivity.

29 Eric A. Hanushek, John F. Kain, and Steven G. Rivkin, "Teachers, Schools, and Academic Achievement," National Bureau of Economic Research, August 1, 1998, nber.org.

and a physically and psychologically healthy home environment where resources like books and academic games are available has far greater influence on his or her educational outcomes than does any aspect of public schooling.[30] This is one of the most consistent patterns in educational research of the past half century: The socioeconomic status of a child's parents is one of the strongest predictors of his or her academic success.

Nevertheless, a 2014 initiative from the Department of Education called "Excellent Educators for All" continues to emphasize the role of the teacher in closing the achievement gap, requiring states to submit "Comprehensive Educator Equity Plans" by April 2015 detailing the steps they take to ensure low-income students and students of color aren't taught by inexperienced or unqualified teachers at higher rates than other children.[31] StudentsFirst, Michelle Rhee's nonprofit, is "driven by the *belief* that every child—regardless of background—can succeed if put in the right school environment," a belief that is delusional in the face of the evidence and cannot therefore be taken in earnest by anyone seeking to transform the education system and improve the lives of American families (my italics).[32]

Bruce Baker, a professor at the Graduate School of Education at Rutgers, found that smaller class sizes, higher

---

30   David C. Berliner and Gene V. Glass, *50 Myths and Lies That Threaten America's Public Schools: The Real Crisis in Education* (New York: Teachers College Press, 2014), 49–54.

31   US Department of Education, "New Initiative to Provide All Students Access to Great Educators," news release, July 7, 2014, ed.gov.

32   studentsfirst.org/OurMission.

teacher salaries (not merit pay), and better instructional materials were also associated with measurable differences in student outcomes. All of these factors are palpably out of the hands of teachers—but none of them have drawn attention from corporate reformers.[33] Former New York City Mayor Michael Bloomberg has said that his ideal education system would require firing half of the city's teachers and paying twice as much to the remainder to teach classes double the size. New York City class sizes rose for the third consecutive time that year, and as of September 2014, they continue to grow.[34] New York City schools have among the highest class sizes in the nation, with 25.5 children in the average elementary or middle school classroom, and 330,000 students in classes of 30 or more during the 2013–14 school year.[35]

How is it that the corporate education reform movement can take so much interest in improving schools while expressing hostility for teachers? The answer, of course, is children. By framing the needs of teachers as intrinsically in opposition to the needs of children, neoliberal education reformers are able to transfer blame from powerful policy makers squarely onto the shoulders of teachers, especially those working in low-income neighborhoods—more often labeled as "failing"

33   Valerie Strauss, "Report: Does Money Matter in Education?," *Answer Sheet* (blog), *Washington Post*, January 6, 2012, washingtonpost.com.
34   Mary Ann Giordano and Anna M. Phillips, "Mayor Hits Nerve in Remarks on Class Sizes and Teachers," *New York Times*, December 2, 2011, nytimes.com; and NYC Department of Education, *2011–12 Preliminary Class Size Report*, November 2011, schools.nyc.gov.
35   Al Baker, "Public Schools in New York City Are Poorer and More Crowded, Budget Agency Finds," *New York Times*, July 1, 2014, nytimes.com.

and closed down for poor performance, with brazen, almost aggressive disregard for those who spend their days there.

In 2011, the NAACP provoked the outrage of New York City Schools Chancellor Dennis Walcott by suing the state Department of Education to prevent twenty-two public schools from being turned to charters. "Right now the UFT [United Federation of Teachers, New York City's major teachers' union] and the NAACP are denying our students quality options," said Walcott. A year later, when the Panel for Education Policy (the New York City School Board) voted to close a Brownsville, Brooklyn,[36] elementary school that had been opened in 2008 to replace another school that was being closed, protest from parents, teachers, and activists was so loud at the town hall meeting that panel members had to wear headphones to hear testimony.[37] Nevertheless, the show went on.

Condoleezza Rice, Mitt Romney, and Arne Duncan have all called education "the civil rights issue of our generation," as if integration of public schools was the singular demand made by activists. In fact, not only was the value of integrating children into a racist school system a point of contention among Black activists during the Civil Rights era, but those who embraced it did so in the context of a larger agenda of

---

36   Just eight miles from Manhattan, Brownsville is one of the poorest neighborhoods in New York City, with about 40 percent of residents living below the poverty line: Mosi Secret, "On the Brink in Brownsville," *New York Times Magazine*, May 1, 2014, nytimes.com.

37   Anna M. Phillips, "City Board Votes to Close 18 Schools and Truncate 5 Amid Protesters' Disruptions," *New York Times*, February 10, 2012, nytimes.com.

justice, dignity, and redistribution of wealth for all people of color, not just Black *children*, with the understanding that we can't change schools without changing society. Corporate education reformers steamroll dissent to the dismantling of worker protections and the shutting down of local schools— attempts to reform schools without addressing fundamental inequalities in the distribution of resources—by rhetorically disconnecting the needs of children from the needs of adults.

That the findings of the California court in the important *Vergara* case, the missions of faux grassroots parent "activist" groups that are actually run by tech billionaires and hedge funders, and federal initiatives for change all narrow in on the role of the teacher in educational outcomes so forcefully, despite decades of policy research concluding that the impact of teachers on children's achievement is minimal, shows us the power of a cultural narrative in which the Teacher Hero or Mother Hero[38] must save the indigent child from a fate of poverty and disaffection through the tool of education.

Helpless to produce the miraculous results expected of them, teachers are found unsatisfactory and immoral, even by their own accounts. This is as bad for the child and her family as it is for the teacher. In a rhetorical sleight of hand, it turns children who have been exploited and oppressed into pathological sufferers defined by their needs. Equality

---

38   The Mother Hero is the preferred beneficiary of global schemes to reduce inequality, such as microfinance, based on presumably innate feminine qualities such as altruism and caregiving. This has resulted in a lot of Girl Power talk, while making women solely responsible for raising the standard of living in their nation-states.

becomes predicated on a moral appeal to those in power ("shocks the conscience"), instead of a demand. Teachers are asked by business reformers to sacrifice themselves in the name of "belt-tightening," for the greater good—for the children—by giving more time and energy to make up for structural deficiencies, as mothers have been asked to do for centuries. As we have seen, the exploitation of women and children and students and teachers is not mutually exclusive, but often interconnected.

In a personal essay, Sarah Blaine, who taught in a rural high school for two years before leaving the classroom to go to law school, describes her reaction to recognizing a former student in a *New York Times* graphic of soldiers killed in Iraq and Afghanistan, on New Year's Day five years later: "[I] didn't know [he'd enlisted]. Because [I'd] copped out and left."[39] She cried for the entire day.

Who accepts responsibility for the life and death of this man? Not the state, with its military-industrial complex and imperialist wars; not the Pentagon, which recruits heavily in economically depressed rural areas,[40] but the woman who taught him English language arts for one year and is racked with guilt half a decade later for "copping out."

When reality fails, as it must, to conform to ideology and the de facto dual system of education is exposed, one for rich children and one for poor children, the result is private shame

---

39   Sarah Blaine, "The Teachers," reproduced in Valerie Strauss, "You Think You Know What Teachers Do. Right? Wrong," *Answer Sheet* (blog), *Washington Post*, February 22, 2014, washingtonpost.com.

40   Ann Scott Tyson, "Youths in Rural U.S. Are Drawn to Military," *Washington Post*, November 4, 2005, washingtonpost.com.

and public outrage—not against structural inequality and dispossession, but against those who have been determined *accountable* for social reproduction. Teachers' ratings are published in the newspaper for all to see and judge, even though educational researchers have been pointing for decades to links between family income, lack of resources in schools serving those families, and race and educational inequality, arguing that we can't expect to change schooling without changing society.[41]

In 2011, Obama's Secretary of Education Arne Duncan complained:

> We've had five decades of reforms, countless studies, water-shed reports like *A Nation at Risk*, and repeated affirmations and commitments from the body politic to finally make education a national priority. And yet we are still waiting for the day when every child in America has a high-quality education that prepares him or her for the future.

We'll be waiting a long time if we expect teachers and mothers to bring it about through sheer force of will.

The right to bear and raise children

To whom, if anyone, does a child belong? Societies answer this question differently at different times, but Americans

---

41   Gary Orfield and Chungmei Lee, *Why Segregation Matters: Poverty and Educational Inequality* (Cambridge, MA: Civil Rights Project, Harvard University, 2005), civilrightsproject.ucla.edu.

have come down firmly in favor of recognizing individual parental authority over the public interest in children's lives. This perspective has roots in the ideals of our Enlightenment-era founders, harmonizing with a legacy of spirited defense of negative freedoms (freedom from the state, for adults at least) over positive freedoms, such as the right of a human being to develop to her fullest potential. It also frames children as the private possessions of their biological or legally adopted parents. In the majority of states, for example, parents are legally entitled to their child's income until they are eighteen, are held accountable for damages to others' property inflicted by their children, and have the right to determine what that child can wear or even say.[42]

The US Supreme Court has consistently upheld child rearing as a constitutionally guaranteed component of the individual's right to life and liberty, recognizing a "private realm of family life which the state cannot enter," even in rulings that effectively broaden civil rights.[43] Courts have interpreted the Fourth and Fifth amendments as protections against government invasion "of the sanctity of a man's home and the privacies of life" (*Boyd v. United States*, 1886), determining that a man ought to have the right to "marry, establish a home and bring up children, to worship God according to the dictates of his own conscience, and generally to enjoy those privileges long recognized as common law essential to

---

42   Children have the right to free speech, but parents can prohibit them from using curse words. Aspen Education Group, "Balancing the Legal Rights of Parents and Teens," aspeneducation.crchealth.com.

43   Justia US Law, "Development of the Right of Privacy," law.justia. com.

the orderly pursuit of happiness by free man" (*Meyer v. Nebraska*, 1923). In *Pierce v. Society of Sisters* (1925), which has been cited as a precedent in over a hundred Supreme Court cases including *Roe v. Wade*, the court ruled that:

> The fundamental theory of liberty upon which all governments in this Union repose excludes any general power of the state to standardize its children by forcing them to accept instruction from public teachers only. The child is not the mere creature of the state; those who nurture him and direct his destiny have the right, coupled with the high duty, to recognize and prepare him for additional obligations.

The court's decision in *Wisconsin v. Yoder* (1972), upholding the right of Amish parents to give their children private schooling, noted that the "primary role of the parents in the upbringing of their children is now established beyond debate as an enduring American tradition." This enduring tradition is apparent even in the terms of debate of one of the court's most radical rulings, *Roe v. Wade*, which legalized abortion in some circumstances on the basis of the individual's right to personal privacy above the state's interest in the potential child—expanding the domain of parental rights from men to mothers and other women (implicitly defined as "not-mothers").

Roe v. Wade altered the power dynamics within the nuclear family while doing little to undermine the nuclear family itself as the primary social unit in the political economy, as radical feminists might have hoped. The court's decision did not recognize a woman's right to freely terminate a pregnancy at any point. Christine Stansell quotes feminist activist Lucinda Cisler "warning with prescience that the battle was not over," since "the concept that fetuses have priority over women was not completely rejected by the court, while the concept of fully human autonomy for women was clearly not affirmed."[44]

More recently, eighty-four members of the House of Representatives including Pete Hoekstra and Michele Bachmann cosponsored a Parental Rights Amendment to the Constitution during the 2013–14 Congress. Backed by conservative organizations including the American Family Association, Concerned Women for America, and Focus on the Family, the amendment would explicate the rights of parents over their children and prevent the United States from observing international laws regarding children's rights.

The United States is one of only three UN members, along with South Sudan and Somalia, that has not yet ratified the UN Convention on the Rights of the Child, a comprehensive framework of children's inalienable rights that includes the right to life—and the responsibility of the state to ensure children's survival and development "to the maximum extent possible"; the right to safety and health services; the freedom to seek and receive information; the right to freedom of

---

44   Christine Stansell, *The Feminist Promise: 1792 to the Present* (New York: Modern Library, 2010).

thought and religion; the right to freely express one's views and be heard in judicial and administrative proceedings; the right to freedom of association and peaceful assembly; the right to protection from illicit transfer abroad; and the right to privacy.[45]

Parentalrights.org, an activist group created to promote the passage of the Parental Rights Amendment, explain their opposition to the ratification of the Convention on the Rights of the Child this way: The treaty may sound good, they say, but it would replace the standard of parental rights "with the 'best interest of the child' standard, which makes government actors, and not parents, ultimately responsible to make final decisions in the care of any child."

They are flatly against what they term "the mandated entitlement" of redistribution of resources—that is, they do not believe they should be obligated to pay tax dollars to provide an adequate standard of living for other people's children. They also object to the outlawing of corporal punishment of children.[46]

The principles behind this staunch resistance to an adequate standard of living for children may be self-explanatory to conservatives, but for others, it requires some analysis. Corey Robin argues in *The Reactionary Mind* that conservatism is a deeply emotional but ultimately rational response to emancipatory movements by those who desire to

---

45   "Convention on the Rights of the Child," Office of the High Commissioner for Human Rights, ohchr.org.
46   "Why We Oppose It—Problems with the CPRD," parentalrights. org.

maintain their privilege. Every once in a while, subordinates rise up and demand not just *liberty* but *equality*, and

> The more profound and prophetic stance on the right has been [John] Adams's. Cede the field of the public, if you must, stand fast in the private. Allow men and women to become democratic citizens of the state; make sure they remain feudal subjects in the family, the factory, and the field. The priority of conservative political argument has been the maintenance of private regimes of power—even at the cost of the strength and integrity of the state.[47]

The political usefulness of creating and maintaining "private regimes of power" amid wide-scale dispossession can be traced back to the origins of industrial capitalism. If, during the transition from feudalism to agrarian and then industrial capitalism, the yeoman was transformed from owner of productive land to alienated wage laborer, he was awarded in turn a domestic sphere imaginatively cut off from the public/economic one, consisting of a wife and children over whom he was master and in whom he found imaginary shelter from the storm of market imperatives—the subject of sentimental dramatizations ever since. A man can be a wage slave at work but rule as an unquestioned king in his home. Thus, as historian Eli Zaretsky has observed, enclosure and the invention of socialized labor led to a split between "the

---

47 Corey Robin, *The Reactionary Mind: Conservatism from Edmund Burke to Sarah Palin* (New York: Oxford University Press, 2011).

realm of wage labor ('work') from domestic production ('family')."[48]

This arrangement, made possible by the family wage and the devaluation of women's work, served as a sort of reparation for the proletarianization and loss of self-determination of a specific class of enfranchised men—a loss that American libertarians still mourn today. "I imagine every one will judge it reasonable, that their children, when little, should look upon their parents as their lords, their absolute governors, and as such stand in awe of them," wrote John Locke, in his parenting guide *Some Thoughts Concerning Education* (1693), in the midst of the enclosure acts and on the brink of the English Agrarian Revolution.

The ideology of the separate spheres was institutionalized and naturalized through culture and politics, its fundamental terms unchallenged until Marxist feminists of the 1960s and 70s reacted against the rendering of women's labor as invisible by demanding (sometimes seriously, sometimes rhetorically) wages for housework, declaring all women housewives, and housewives "indispensible to capitalist production." At the same time, radical feminists like Shulamith Firestone and Ellen Willis pointed out that *the personal* was political. As feminist activists Mariarosa Dalla Costa and Selma James wrote in 1972 in "The Power of Women and the Subversion of the Community":

---

48   Eli Zaretsky, *Capitalism, the Family and Personal Life* (New York: Harper & Row, 1976).

Women are trying to break down the division that has been made between the father and the children and between the mother and the father. The privilege that society has given the man, women are not allowing him. It is a privilege that he suffers by as well as she. Men know little about their children, are not close to them, and don't know what giving time and work to a child gives back to you. Men feel that supporting a child is all they have to do to get the love of their child and the respect of their wife.[49]

"The Power of the Women and the Subversion of the Community" saw schooling as intrinsically like factory labor, capital "excluding" men and then children from the home, and advocated for the refusal of work altogether. Mainstream second-wave feminists, on the other hand, demanded expanded legal rights and increased access to paid work in the public sphere. Thus in the twentieth century, as Zaretsky writes, "family" came to be identified as the "life" component in "work/life balance," an authentic domain that parents must steal time away from the office to participate in.

This is what the "culture wars" were all about. Men resisted women's elbowing into roles of power in the public/economic sphere because they accurately recognized in second-wave feminism a threat to their long-established dominion over the domestic sphere. Women gained

---

49   Mariarosa Dalla Costa and Selma James, "The Power of Women and the Subversion of the Community," in Selma James, *Sex, Race and Class: The Perspective of Winning: A Selection of Writings 1952–2011* (Oakland, CA: PM Press, 2012).

recognition if not equality as workers and potential bread-winners, entering the labor force in record numbers. Children became "latchkey" kids and juvenile delinquents roaming the streets in gangs.

To be sure, working-class women and children had been a part of the labor force long before the publication of the *Feminine Mystique*—a reality that many second-wave feminists did not adequately take into account—however, the statistics bear out the cultural metaphor of a mass exodus from homemaking to the workplace. While women comprised just 18 percent of the labor force in 1900, they made up nearly half of it in 2009. In 1900, only 20 percent of women worked. Over the period from 1970 to 1985, the percentage of women sixteen years and over in the labor force increased to more than 40 percent, and from 1997 to 2008, to 60 percent.[50]

Conservatives reacted to this shift by mounting a sadistic, determined, and organized counterrevolution, epitomized by the moral policing of mothers (especially single mothers) and the Satanic Panic of the 1980s, during which hundreds of day-care owners were tried and imprisoned on charges of ritualistic child abuse, only to be proven innocent years later. The conservative preoccupation with nuclear families still holds politicians in thrall today: In January 2014, Senator Rand Paul suggested cutting government benefits for unwed mothers who continue to have children. "Maybe we have to

---

50   AFL-CIO Department for Professional Employees, "Professional Women: Vital Statistics," Fact Sheet 2010, National Committee on Pay Equity, pay-equity.org; "Women in the Labor Force, 1970–2009," *Economics Daily*, January 5, 2011, bls.gov.

say 'enough's enough, you shouldn't be having kids after a certain amount,'" he argued. As Bryce Covert of *ThinkProgress* points out, sixteen American states actually have caps on assistance in place that do not give additional TANF funds to expectant parents who are already receiving assistance.[51] On the other hand, liberals attempted to reconcile and integrate feminist critique into preexisting social structures. The idea was that men would be asked to share the responsibilities of the private sphere with women, and women would be allowed to share economic power with men.

Today, the maintenance of the home as a private regime of power for male—and as we shall see, to varying degrees, female—*parents* distinct from the state is critical to the platforms of both American conservatives and liberals, who deal with anxieties about child-rearing as women return to work in different ways (recall Tipper Gore's crusade for Parental Advisory warnings on CDs). Despite feminist interventions, Americans remain strongly committed to viewing children as the private concern of the nuclear family and child care as a personal rather than political problem. The conflict between "family" and "life" was still broadly conceptualized as an individual balancing act, but it was one faced by nearly every American family.

The balancing act is frequently dramatized in culture: Its main characters are an ambitious, workaholic father—whose work is represented as an egoistic addiction rather than a financial imperative—and a doe-eyed, patient, but inevitably

---

51   Bryce Covert, "Senator Floats Idea to Penalize Low-Income Women Who Have Children," *ThinkProgress*, January 29, 2014, thinkprogress.org.

fed-up mother. Often the film opens at the moment they are on the verge of divorce.

In *Kramer vs. Kramer* (both the highest-grossing and Oscar-winning film of 1979), Meryl Streep's character Joanna, an unhappy stay-at-home mom who walks out on her marriage and young son at the beginning of the film, encapsulates the mission of conventional second-wave feminism perfectly in one breathless sentence: "In California, I think I found myself. I got myself a job. I got myself a therapist." Later, when she returns to take part in a custody battle and is announced as the first witness, her ex-husband's lawyer leans over to him and whispers, "Real direct. Motherhood . . . they're going right for the throat." The film details the emotional struggle of mothers and fathers as women entered the workforce. Joanna tells the court,

> Just because I'm a woman, don't I have a right to the same hopes and dreams as a man? Don't I have a right to a life of my own? Is that so awful? . . . I left my child—I know there is no excuse for that. But since then, I have gotten help. I have worked hard to become a whole human being. I don't think I should be punished for that.[52]

Nevertheless, the psychic need to keep the family unit intact is a prevailing theme in American politics and culture. Where children are legally connected to their parents' private property

---

52 Robert Benton, *Kramer vs. Kramer*, 1979, Internet Movie Script Database, imsdb.com.

through a decentralized system of funding schools through local and state property taxes (in the United States, only about 10 to 15 percent of funding for public schools comes from the federal government), and given the disparities within and between districts, it is evident that a mother arrested for sending her child to a school district in which she does not have residence is not merely being punished for falsifying documents, but for "stealing education," for *taking* resources she hasn't (according to the logic of capitalism) paid for, and to which her child is therefore not entitled. These include not just books and computers, but a safe environment free from concentrated poverty, where parents have the financial and political power to hold reformers accountable. It is impossible to imagine a wealthy suburban town hall meeting where school board members put headphones on to drown out protestors.

Ohio mother Kelley Williams-Bolar was handcuffed and jailed for nine days in 2010 for "records tampering," using her father's address to enroll her daughters in a different school district than the one in which she resided, out of concern for their safety.[53] In 2012, Tanya McDowell, a Connecticut mother, was charged with first-degree larceny, having allegedly "stolen" over $15,686 in educational services by enrolling her son in Norwalk Public Schools using her babysitter's address (McDowell was homeless at the time). McDowell's son visited the babysitter daily, but his biological mother spent most nights sleeping in a different district.

---

53   Timothy Williams, "Jailed for Switching Her Daughters' School District," *New York Times*, September 26, 2011, nytimes.com.

Apparently, the sacred right to bear and raise children without government interference does not extend in practice to Black mothers or poor mothers. In April of 2014, thirty-five-year-old Shanesha Taylor pleaded not guilty to charges of felony child abuse for leaving her two sons unsupervised in her Dodge Durango for over an hour during a job interview, after her child-care arrangements fell through. A woman on her lunch break who noticed the children sweating profusely in the backseat that March afternoon had called the cops. According to the testimony of the firefighters who arrived on the scene, the temperature of the car was over 100 degrees and the youngest, an infant, was crying hysterically.

On the *Today* show, Taylor called the incident a moment of desperation. She asked reporters,

Do you pass up the interview that you know is going to save your family? Do you pass up the interview you know is going to give you a future? Or do I stay here and do I care for the children?

She pointed out the impossibility of her situation to the embarrassment even of Fox News and the *Daily News*, which fired back five months later with the headline, "Arizona Mom Who Left Kids in Hot Car Spent Thousands of Dollars of Donation Money 'To Finish Her Baby Daddy's Rap Album': Ex-Pal."[54]

---

54 Emanuella Grinberg, "When Justice Is 'Merciful' in Child Abuse Cases," CNN, August 7, 2014, cnn.com; David Boroff, "Arizona Mom Who Left Kids in Hot Car Spent Thousands of Dollars of Donation Money 'To

That summer, Debra Harrell was arrested for letting her nine-year-old play alone at a playground rather than forcing her to sit in the McDonald's where she worked all day. Her child was placed in foster care. The same month, a Florida mom, Nicole Gainey, was arrested for child neglect, a felony, after police found her son playing in the park less than a mile from her home. On the report, the police officer noted that "numerous sex offenders reside in the vicinity," echoing the concerns of the moral panic directed toward child-care facilities in the 1980s. The case is still open, and as of August 2014, the Department of Children and Families was not planning on dropping charges.[55]

Another mother, Kim Brooks, was cited by police for "contributing to the delinquency of a minor" and "rendering him in need of services" when she left her son alone in her car while running into the grocery store. He didn't want to go in and she didn't feel like dealing with a tantrum that day. But when a Good Samaritan called the cops, she had to fight for years to prove that she was a fit mother.[56]

Reflecting on the decision, Brooks writes, "I did what I'd been doing every minute of every day since having children, a constant, never-ending risk-benefit analysis." She was ashamed at the results, but she also points out that statistically speaking, it would take 750,000 years for a child left alone in

Finish Her Baby Daddy's Rap Album': Ex-Pal," *Daily News*, November 17, 2014, nydailynews.com.

55   Elizabeth Harrington, "Port St. Lucie Mom Arrested after Allowing Her 7-Year-Old Son to Go to a Nearby Park Alone," WPTV Newschannel 5, July 28, 2014, wptv.com.

56   Harrell and Taylor are Black. Gainey and Brooks are white.

a public space to be snatched by a stranger, whereas 300 children are injured in traffic accidents every day. Note how the fulfillment of Brooks's needs are perceived, both by her and the state, as in conflict with the needs of her child ("I felt I'd put my child at risk for my own momentary convenience"), and how she is disciplined for seemingly putting hers first. The riskiest thing she did that day could have been driving to the supermarket, but what she was punished for was leaving her son alone unsupervised in the world.

How is it that social conservatives can advocate for a focus on the family while violently hating women? That is, *some women* and *some mothers*—for they do not hate Nancy Reagan in her demure Chanel tweed suits, nor Phyllis Schlafly with her call for men to "stop taking our privileges," nor Sarah Palin, who will be a fixture in the American conservative imagination long after John McCain. But social conservatives and the "free-market" American state have repeatedly stigmatized and criminalized poor women, angry women, Black women, women with demands, "single" women, and women who refuse to be mothers or who reject motherhood or worst of all, who "fail" as mothers.

Three of the four instances of neglect charges I've described (all of them news last year) involve a mother who would have preferred to leave her child in the care of another person whether for an hour-long job interview or a ten-minute errand, but did not have the necessary supports to do so, and the fourth involves a dispute over the extent to which a child needs surveillance—all four women spent time in court or jail. Two of the four women were Black, and the majority were working class or unemployed. Not only did the state intervene in the lives of these women and children in direct contradiction to libertarian fantasies and American legal precedent; it intervened with the unambiguous intention of rescuing the children from their hapless and negligent mothers, rather than of providing much-needed social supports. Then what? What will be done with all of these rescued children?

In a *National Review* symposium, "The War on Poverty at 50," Michael J. Petrilli of the Hoover Institution and Thomas B. Fordham Institute proposed that what "our young people" need are stable parents with resources and commitment, even if it means taking them out of "dysfunctional families and communities" and transporting them to environments that

as President George W. Bush would say, "touch their hearts." The most promising among these are schools of choice that prepare students academically and vocationally—so that they might see a future for themselves beyond the walls of poverty—but also emotionally, socially, and spiritually . . . Such schools should be measured by the degree to which their graduates are college- and career-ready, yes, but also fatherhood-ready and motherhood-ready.[57]

For their part, poor families should, according to Petrilli, make

---

57   "The War on Poverty at 50," *National Review*, January 8, 2014, nationalreview.com.

good decisions daily about what they will or won't expect
of their kids; the time they will or won't spend with them;
the books they will or won't read to them; the experiences
they will or won't provide. It shouldn't be controversial to
say, then, that many poor parents struggle to make these
good decisions, often because they themselves are still
growing up and are trying to do the job alone.[58]

Petrilli's solution for reducing intergenerational poverty?
Everyone must follow "a simple rule": Don't have kids until
you are ready to provide for them, emotionally and
financially.

In the context of a racist, sexist, and increasingly class-
stratified society, women—particularly, women of color,
who receive harsher punishments for education "theft" and
child "neglect"—continue to be held responsible by the state
in the same manner and for the same things that they have
long been answerable for as mothers: the moral education
and salvation of children.[59] Even if the doctrine of the separate spheres has been theoretically challenged, the sexual
division of labor is alive and well. Though feminists successfully made the question of "who will do the shit work"[60]

58   Ibid.
59   "Fast Facts: Teacher Trends," National Center for Education
Statistics, nces.ed.gov; Thomas E. Glass, "Where Are All the Women
Superintendents?," AASA, the School Superintendents Association, aasa.
org. For example, only 30 percent of high school principals are women, in a
profession that has otherwise been dominated by women since the turn of
the century.
60   Ellen Willis, "Up from Radicalism: A Feminist Journal," in *The
Essential Ellen Willis*, ed. Nona Willis Aronowitz, 5–19 (Minneapolis, MN:

contested territory in the middle decades of the twentieth century, the conflict remains unresolved and continues to be treated by American society as a personal challenge to be solved by individual nuclear families, "on their own time" and through their own means.

Neoliberalism, a political philosophy that prioritizes "freeing" markets from regulation and privatizing public services, has transformed the social role of the child and caregiver. Instead of liberating mothers and teachers, it has further strapped them with the obligation to compensate for the state's failure to provide basic public services and blaming them when—due to structural reasons—they can't.

The United States is one of three countries in the world that doesn't require employers to offer parental leave for the birth of a child (Swaziland and Papua New Guinea are the others), and it is mothers, not fathers, who take on the double shift in place of a collective solution to the rise of the dual-earner family—not that you would know it given Petrilli's argument.[61]

Working mothers of all classes put in an approximately eighty-hour workweek including responsibilities for waged work and child care, longer than anyone else in the economy, and as the private costs of raising children—that is, the costs of health care, college, housing, and other essential provisions—have risen steadily throughout the past half century, women have paid for them through their double and

University of Minnesota Press, 2014).
    61   Arlie Russell Hochschild and Anne Machung, *The Second Shift: Working Parents and the Revolution at Home* (New York: Viking, 1989).

sometimes triple shift.[62] In the United States, child care is regarded as a personal matter and offered by some employers as a benefit to attract talent, leading to a de facto apartheid system of child care stratified by race and class, to match our segregated K–12 school system. Mothers who are unable, due to structural reasons, to fill the gaps—usually the poorest women—are criminalized.

Parents and teachers are important figures in the lives of children and should offer them love, warmth, guidance, and protection. But it is unreasonable to expect either motherhood or public schooling to rectify a collective problem that is woven into the fabric of American society. Mayor Bill de Blasio's justification for keeping NYC public schools open in treacherous weather conditions in the winter of 2014— that for some children, missing a day of school means missing breakfast and lunch—makes visible the immense and dangerous pressure put on public schools to serve as a social safety net in the absence of meaningful public welfare programs.

Choice policies such as vouchers and charter schools have been put forward by corporate reformers as a solution to the outrageous inequities of the American educational system, with convenient ideological benefits: They appeal to the ingrained American distrust of federal intervention in parenting and tie deregulation to equality. Choice advocates argue that charter schools and voucher programs benefit

---

62 Ann Crittenden, *The Price of Motherhood: Why the Most Important Job in the World Is Still the Least Valued* (New York: Metropolitan, 2001).

"disadvantaged" students by giving their parents the same ability to choose between options.

But researchers have found convincing evidence that charter schools increase the overall level of race and class segregation in the school system.[63] Schools that control their admissions are less likely to admit low-income students, English-language learners, and students with special needs— all of whom cost more to educate. Further, when school choice is available, parents, *especially* white parents, "typically choose schools in which their children will not be in a racial or socioeconomic minority ... Highly educated parents are especially likely to focus on student demographics."[64] Parents with higher socioeconomic backgrounds are also the ones with the time to hire a babysitter and sit in on a kindergarten or middle school admissions workshop that will give them the information needed to ascertain differences between options and decide on the best. School choice pits families in competition with one another for seats at public schools; it does not equalize opportunity.

Child-rearing as a private enterprise

Today, nearly half of American children born to parents with low incomes grow into adults with low incomes, and 40 percent of children born to wealthy parents become

---

63   Gary Orfield and Erica Frankenberg, *Educational Delusions?: Why Choice Can Deepen Inequality and How to Make Schools Fair* (Berkeley, CA: University of California Press, 2012).

64   Jennifer L. Hochschild and Nathan B. Scovronick, *The American Dream and the Public Schools* (New York: Oxford University Press, 2004).

high-income adults. In the United States, which has based much of its social safety net on educational mobility, the ability to do better than one's parents by completing more years of schooling did indeed rise between 1947 and 1977, but it has decreased sharply since. Correlation of educational attainment between parents and children is now higher in the United States than in European countries, particularly Nordic countries, where a tiny fraction of low-income children becomes low-income adults.[65] As Richard Wilkinson, coauthor of *The Spirit Level*, has said, "If Americans want to live the American dream, they should go to Denmark."[66]

Upward mobility has always been the exception to the rule—children born to families in the bottom income quintile have about a 6 percent chance of making it to the top income quintile in their lifetimes—but unfortunately it is a fantasy on which United States welfare programs are now based.[67] Never has pulling oneself up by one's bootstraps been more plainly a cruel fiction than when prescribed as a policy regime for large swaths of the population. Under Clinton, who delivered on his promise to "end welfare as we know it," direct aid—itself hardly redistributive—has been replaced with punitive welfare-to-work   programs   emphasizing   personal

65   Miles Corak, *Do Poor Children Become Poor Adults? Lessons from a Cross-Country Comparison of Generational Earnings Mobility* (Bonn, Germany: IZA, 2006).

66   Richard G. Wilkinson and Kate Pickett, *The Spirit Level: Why Greater Equality Makes Societies Stronger* (New York: Bloomsbury, 2010).

67   Julia B. Isaacs, "Economic Mobility of Families across Generations," in *Getting Ahead or Losing Ground: Economic Mobility in America*, eds. Ron Haskins, Julia B. Isaacs, and Isabel V. Sawhill (Washington, DC: Brookings Institution, 2012).

responsibility. In 1996, Aid to Families with Dependent Children (AFDC) become temporary (TANF), and continuous access to government transfers became contingent on filing a tax return (Earned Income Tax Credit, or EITC).

Using data from tax records, economist Thomas Piketty shows that both capital income and earned income have grown for the richest families to the extent that in the America of 2010, like the Gilded Age Europe of 1910, the top 1 percent owns the same share of income as the bottom 50 percent, and the top 10 percent own the same share as the bottom 90 percent. Since the 1970s, real wages for workers have increased little or decreased, while wages for the top 1 percent have risen 165 percent. Seventy percent of the income of the top 0.01 percent is from capital income, not wages.[68] A similarly unprecedented survey of data from nearly all math and reading scores over the past forty years conducted by Sean Reardon of the Center for Education Policy Analysis at Stanford has determined that during the same period of time (since the 1970s) "trends in the test scores of low- and high-income children parallel those of income itself, with income-based gaps in test scores now twice as large as test score gaps between African Americans and whites."[69] Even as racial gaps in test scores decreased in the years since *Brown v. Board of Education*, the income-based gap in test scores has risen.[70] More

68   Paul Krugman, "Why We're in a New Gilded Age," *New York Review of Books*, May 8, 2014, nybooks.com, a review of Thomas Piketty, *Capital in the Twenty-First Century*, trans. Arthur Goldhammer (Cambridge, MA: Belknap Press/Harvard University Press, 2014).

69   Greg J. Duncan and Richard J. Murnane, eds., "Introduction: The American Dream Then and Now," in *Whither Opportunity?: Rising Inequality, Schools, and Children's Life Chances*, Russel Sage Foundation, 10.

70   Sean F. Reardon, "The Widening Income Achievement Gap,"

profoundly than ever, and in more ways than ever, class determines the life paths open to a child.

The difference between Dickensian England and the present-day United States is that few rich people recognize that they have won the birth lottery. Instead, as political scientist John Gerring has noted, "poverty" is ascertained as a national crisis, a disease. In the language of philanthropy, capitalism is transformed from a cause to a solution. Conservatives punish; liberals forgive; neoliberals solve. Framed this way, it makes sense that businessmen want to lift children out of the blight of "poverty," rather than throw them down in it Oliver Twist–style. Poverty pathologizes people who are losing in capitalism rather than concrete economic sources: "There are victims, but no victimizers."[71] The language of "poverty" keeps us from questioning and critiquing our economic system in a way that "wealth inequality" and "class disparity"—or class war—does not.

But it is a class war in which we find ourselves, involving not just men and not just women, but children. Researchers at the Russell Sage Foundation have documented a shift in the way American children are raised that parallels the political-economic context in which they grow up.[72] Over the period from 1972 to 1988, as society became more economically stratified and surges in GDP began to benefit an increasingly smaller percentage of high-income families, schools also became more economically segregated.

Educational Leadership 70, no. 8 (May 2013): 10–16.

71   John Gerring, *Party Ideologies in America 1828–1996* (Cambridge, UK: Cambridge University Press, 2001).

72   Duncan and Murnane, *Whither Opportunity*.

A study by labor economists Joseph G. Altonji and Richard Mansfield finds that the sorting of children into class-segregated schools intensified during the 1980s.[73]

At the same time, spending on child-enrichment goods and services has soared for families in the top income quintiles. Introducing work by policy researchers Neeraj Kaushal, Katherine Magnuson, and Jane Waldfogel, Greg Duncan and Richard Murnane observe, "In the period from 1972 to 1973, high-income families spent about $2,700 more per year on child enrichment than did low-income families," but by 2005 to 2006, "this gap had nearly tripled, to $7,500."[74] Meredith Phillips estimates that from birth to age six, children from affluent families have spent 1,300 more hours in environments beside their home, school, or day care than children from low-income families. Wealthy parents have the luxury of *time* to impart knowledge essential to understanding science and social studies to their children beginning in early childhood through exposure to travel, museums, and even simple excursions like going to the supermarket or the post office.[75]

Given this data, it's not surprising that the first known use of the word "helicopter parent" is in 1989. The fear

---

73 Joseph G. Altonji and Richard Mansfield, "The Role of Family, School, and Community Characteristics in Inequality in Education and Labor-Market Outcomes," in Duncan and Murnane, *Whither Opportunity?*, 339–59.

74 Duncan and Murnane, "Introduction," in Duncan and Murnane, *Whither Opportunity?*; Neeraj Kaushal, Katherine Magnuson, and Jane Waldfogel, "How Is Family Income Related to Investments in Children's Learning?" in Duncan and Murnane, *Whither Opportunity?*

75 Meredith Phillips, "Parenting, Time Use, and Disparities in Academic Outcomes," in Duncan and Murnane, *Whither Opportunity?*

felt by parents of all classes that their children's class status is more precarious is real, even among the middle and upper classes. "Family" continues to be a sentimental concept imagined as a refuge from the wild and awful world of autocratic workplaces, but its project has become protecting and preparing offspring for the cutthroat global economy.

The contemporary family has become a competitive economic unit not only distinct from, but actively *in conflict* with the larger society. The idea of "finding yourself," "getting a job," and "getting a therapist" (to use *Kramer vs. Kramer*'s neat summary) has been increasingly important in American society since the rise of psychology and consumer culture—now the cultivation of a personal identity for one's *children* is also essential to ensuring adult success (and the transmission of privilege across the generations).

After all, childhood is expensive, so it must be an investment. Since 1960, the US Department of Agriculture has prepared an annual estimate of the cost of raising a child. Parents are expected to spend $245,340 to raise a child born in 2013. A flyer/PSA released by the department depicts an imaginary online shopping website modeled on Amazon. com, with the image of a baby priced at "US $245,340" and a mouse arrow hovering ominously over the phrase "Add to family?" Under a "Details" section, the breakdown of costs shows percentages allocated to housing, food, transportation, clothing, health care, child care and education, and miscellaneous. College is "Not included." The USDA has also helpfully provided a Cost of Raising a Child Calculator, which allows parents to create their own individualized estimate based on the household income, marital status, number of children, region, and budget. Parents are thus encouraged to think of the act of reproduction as above all a personal economic choice.[76]

There's an array of tools that promise to help mom and dad raise an intellectual, worldly child in the most efficient way possible. An American-based range of BPA-free toys created with the input of child development experts and sold in over seventy countries called Sassy Baby includes a "developmental insight" and "interaction ideas," with every product. For example, the sensory gym "inspires baby to learn and grow" by incorporating a variety of textures and colors.[77] Interaction ideas include allowing your baby to play with the hanging toys, pointing out the different toys at the end of the arches, and clapping when she reaches for them. As an added bonus, the company asserts, "our passion for fashion assures today's mom that her baby will be *just like her*: fun, savvy, smart . . . SASSY!" Strollers, one of the first items to become a status symbol of the new parenthood when *Sex and the City* writers committed to making one of the characters a Brooklyn mom five seasons in, are sold in premium versions by "Dutch mobility company" Bugaboo, with lots of marketing materials

---

76   Mark Lino, "Expenditures on Children by Families, 2013," US Department of Agriculture, Center for Nutrition Policy and Promotion, no. 1528–2013 (2014). Report, infographic, and calculator are available at cnpp.usda.gov.

77   "80322 Sassy Sensory Gym," sassybaby.com.

about exploring the world and no mention of what is presumably being carried (or concealed?).

South Africa–based Bumbo sells baby seats that encourage practice of postural head and trunk control and a crawl ball advertised as stimulating hand-eye coordination and motor skills, all in the name of *protecting your most valuable asset*. In fact, you'd be hard-pressed to find something that doesn't stimulate the curiosity or inspire the development of hand-eye coordination of "your most valuable asset."

For a few dollars, a nursery can be equipped with plastic blocks in different colors and textures, homemade or store-bought rattles, crayons, chalk, cookie cutters, play-doh, markers, sand and string. Tearing construction paper is a challenging task for a two year-old, which helps develop fine motor skills, as is gathering leaves or cutting with scissors, which builds hand-eye coordination. Babies do not need to be inspired to grow; *they grow*. What baby humans need more than anything is as simple as what any mammal needs: comfort.

Through the consciousness-raising of second-wave feminism, the joys and struggles of parenting have been brought from the privacy of the home into the fore of public life with eager irreverence. The young children of the wealthy are increasingly diverse portfolios of applications to private schools, enrichment classes, play dates, and nanny shares. These little Einsteins go on to attend prestigious high schools and Ivy League colleges. But it starts in preschool. A whole culture has risen around the cultivation of the child into a successful adult, equipped for the global economy. Its language is English plus Spanish or Mandarin; its literature is the mommy blog.

Working-class children, on the other hand, are objects of suspicion defined by what is perceived, within the economic superstructure, as a lack—of high-enough test scores, of self-confidence, or the inclination and facility to self-regulate behavior. Childhood is now a curated experience for the rich, and a desperate challenge full of lotteries and high stakes for the middle-class and working-class families who aspire toward upward mobility. But it is not a particularly pleasurable one anymore.

All the anxious messaging around children as fun, smart, savvy, adventurous assets is a response to the intensifying economic stratification that leaves parents desperate to give their children an edge. Parents' energies are absorbed by their children's needs and schedules with a totality that is monolithic and exhausting. It's not a choice. It's a financial imperative: Middle-class families recognize, implicitly if not explicitly, that their children are born with economic advantages, and as socioeconomic stratification intensifies, there is less room for mistakes than ever. Brian Jones, a former public school teacher for almost a decade as well as a parent activist who recently ran for lieutenant governor of New York, told me in an interview:

> Parents' willingness to embrace these uber-strict test regimes for their very small children even though we know that it makes those children anxious and upset is connected to the fact that the parents feel and know that

the labor market is tightening and shows that their children's [prospects] are tightening. If they knew that the kid was going to be OK; if $15 was the minimum wage and you could go to college for free, everybody has health care, there's plenty of affordable housing—if they just knew that the kid was going to *be OK*, there would be way less hysterical pressure of making your five-year-old jump through that standardized test hoop.

Childhood has been reconceived, not as a time to compensate for the alienated labor of adult life, but a time to prepare for adult life. The rapidly intensifying stratification not just among the rich and poor in America, but even among those within the top 1 percent (the top 0.01 percent have gained more than the rest of the top 1 percent, which has concrete consequences in rich and middle-class parents' perceptions and behavior toward their children), means that rich and middle-class families accurately perceive the cultivation of their children, the constant search for the competitive edge, as essential to ensuring their children access as adults to the knowledge professions rather than offshored and devalued vocational work.

"I see both sides of the choice thing," Jones said.

Having choice is empowering and sense. I get the allure that wealthy people always have choices. The problem is that with that you lose rights, sometimes, with more choices. You become a customer instead of a citizen. I feel both dimensions of it.

As a New York City parent applying to schools for his kindergarten-age daughter (as is required of all families now),

> I have choices, but I don't have any guarantees. I don't have much redress if I don't get my choice. And the schools, especially the charter schools, also have choice in a sense for them even more so because they can un-choose you. Now the deal we have with Kindergarten Connect system [New York City's automated system for matching applicants with schools], after you do your research and you make your choices, it kicks out a single school and then it's take it or leave it, so that's pretty frustrating.

The system again leads to individual responses: Parents appeal to the government to have their children's placement changed. Naturally, the stronger your network and the more time you have, the more likely this is to happen. But crucially, parents no longer respond to the state collectively—they are atomized as consumers.

Compare this to the way that babies are welcomed in Finland, a country that ranks near the very top in both test scores and wealth equality. Instead of a calculator tool to "help you plan better for overall expenses including food, or to purchase adequate life insurance" in preparation for baby, the Finnish state has since 1938 offered expectant parents the choice between a box of clothes, sheets, and toys or a cash grant worth US$190 by the government for supplies.[78] Ninety-five percent of Finnish people choose the box, which is filled with diapers and ointment; clothes including onesies, a snowsuit and hat, a light hooded suit and knit hat, mittens, booties, leggings in various colors and patterns, booties, overalls, socks, and a balaclava; bath needs including a hooded bath towel, nail scissors, hairbrush, toothbrush, and washcloths; and various other essentials including a thermometer, a teething toy, a picture book, bra pads, and condoms.

The box comes filled with a mattress, sleeping bag, and bedding, and can be reused for sleeping. It is a symbolic demonstration of the country's commitment to giving all children an equal start, but it was implemented for entirely practical reasons. A Finnish parent reflected on the experience receiving his child's box to *BBC News*:

> This felt to me like evidence that someone cared, someone wanted our baby to have a good start in life. And now when I visit friends with young children it's nice to see we share some common things. It strengthens that feeling that we are all in this together.[79]

What is at stake when some American children go to school hungry and others go to school in $1,000 Bugaboo strollers? Under the "do what you love" ethos of neoliberal

---

78   Helena Lee, "Why Finnish Babies Sleep in Cardboard Boxes," *BBC News*, June 4, 2013, bbc.com.
79   Ibid.

capitalism, life paths prescribed by class but framed as parental choices—*Public or private? Gifted and talented, general, or special education?*—segregate American children from birth through adolescence and into adulthood as never before, reformulating their upbringings into private family projects and education as a competitive "hunger games" for the material resources and social connections required to secure economic success.

In an important study of eighty poor, working-class, and middle-class Black and white American families with elementary-school-aged children,[80] sociologist Annette Lareau observed and discussed child-rearing practices with kids, mothers, fathers, grandparents, aunts, uncle, cousins, etc. Since pop culture is essentially bourgeois culture, Lareau's study is, by contrast, an unprecedented and attentive record of the values of American working-class and poor families in the 1990s. This is particularly significant given the violent, disapproving caricatures of working-class and poor people by domestic policy "reformers" during that period. Lareau found that—contrary to the welfare queen stereotype—middle-class, working-class, and poor mothers were all involved in "intensive mothering" and expressed beliefs in the importance of showing love and warmth to their children. "There were episodes of laughter, emotional connection, and happiness as well as quiet comfort in every family" that appeared "deeply meaningful to both children and parents in all social classes," she writes.

---

80   Annette Lareau, *Unequal Childhoods: Class, Race, and Family Life* (Berkeley, CA: University of California Press, 2003).

There were, however, a few fundamental differences among poor and working-class families and middle-class families. Some rituals and perspectives cohered strongly by class:

> The role of race was less powerful than I had expected. In terms of the areas this book has focused on—how children spend their time, the way parents use language and discipline in the home, the nature of the families' social connections, and the strategies used for intervening in institutions—white and Black parents engaged in very similar, often identical practices with their children. As the children age, the relative importance of race in their daily lives is likely to increase . . . In fourth grade, however, in very central ways, race mattered less in children's daily lives than did their social class. Black and white middle-class children were given enormous amounts of individualized attention, with their parents organizing their own time around their children's leisure activities. This prioritizing profoundly affected parents' leisure time. In these situations, race made little to no difference . . . It was the middle-class children, Black and white, who squabbled and fought with their siblings and talked back to their parents. These behaviours were simply not tolerated in working-class and poor families, Black or white.

White and Black middle-class parents most often engaged in what Lareau calls "concerted cultivation," adult-facilitated recognition and development of a child's individual talents with classes and lessons, while working-class and poor parents tended to nurture, support, and reflect on the "accomplishment of natural growth." In these families, parent-initiated hobbies were rare, and the preferred mode of speaking to children is directives. A sense of entitlement—being encouraged to question and negotiate with adults, for example—distinctive to middle-class children (and important in securing financial success in American "meritocracy") is trained from birth. Working-class children had strong ties to siblings and extended family and took ownership of their own play, but were actively encouraged to distrust authority figures such as teachers and doctors. This has profound implications for the children's functioning in middle-class institutions, and the rewards they receive.

It's no accident that while the United States offered minimal to nonexistent support for families in comparison to European social democracies, it was the first to implement (according to Stansell) "one of the most liberal abortion laws in the world." Indeed, Justice Harry Blackmun, the chief justice of the Supreme Court in the *Roe v. Wade* case, observed that, "maternity, or additional offspring, may force upon the woman a distressful life and future." If maternity is the "natural" role of a woman, how is it that it could cause her a distressful life? The issue is not whether the woman in question would or would not like to carry the child to term, but whether she can afford to—what would happen to her financial prospects if she did.

There is a fundamental contradiction in what are termed family values and the social supports that are provided for

American women and children as a whole, which Toni Morrison confronts in an interview quoted at length in Nina Power's *One-Dimensional Woman*, which I will excerpt here briefly. When a reporter asked Morrison about the fate of unwed teenage mothers, insisting that they had not had time to "find out if they had special abilities and talents," Morrison replied:

> The child's not going to hurt them . . . They're not babies . . . They can [go on] to be teachers. They can be brain surgeons. We have to help them become brain surgeons. That's my job. I want to take them all in my arms and say, "Your baby is beautiful and so are you and, honey, you can do it. And when you want to be a brain surgeon, call me—I will take care of your baby." That's the attitude you have to have about human life. But we don't want to pay for it.

In fact, Americans pay very dearly for children, but only for those children they regard as *theirs*—children who *belong* to them.

"Every Child Should Have a Hundred Parents"

In her bestselling book, *No Kids: 40 Good Reasons Not to Have Children*, French mother of three Corinne Maier mocks the gauntlet of modern parenthood, invoking couples (at least half seriously) to reject the role—"always on call, smiling, attentive, teacherly, and responsible. Is there anything you won't do to guarantee the 'happiness' and 'fulfillment' of the kids?'"—in favor of self-fulfillment, sex, fun, the joy of quiet dinners, and, if you're a woman, your career. "The education of children has become a sacrament: society demands of modern parents a level of performance worthy of Superman or Superwoman," she adds. "All that for *kids?* Honestly, is it really worth it? The only solution is contraception."[81]

Nina Power's consideration of the scandal of (French) women's *refusal of motherhood as mothers* "towards a queer maternity?" is more interesting than Maier's book—which, from an American perspective, at least, hits far too close to home.[82] Refusal of motherhood does not necessarily read as refusal of the social order in the American context, since American politicians are vigilantly against certain women *becoming* mothers. As recently as 2008, a Louisiana Republican in the House of Representatives, John LaBruzzo, floated the idea of paying poor women $1,000 to have their tubes tied. ("What I'm really studying is any and all possibilities that we can reduce the number of people that are going from generational welfare to generational welfare."[83])

Maier's satirical suggestion of contraception as the solution to the burdens of child rearing is too similar to our actual economic   policy   (conservatives   would   substitute

81   Corinne Maier, *No Kids: 40 Good Reasons Not to Have Children*, trans. Patrick Watson (Toronto: McClelland & Stewart, 2009), 2.

82   Not incidentally, the same can be said of Maier's *Bonjour Laziness: Why Hard Work Doesn't Pay* (New York: Vintage, 2006).

83   Satyam Khanna, "Louisiana Lawmaker Advocates Eugenics: Sterilize Poor Women, Encourage Rich to Procreate," *ThinkProgress*, September 24, 2008, thinkprogress.org.

"contraception" with abstinence or sterilization) to read as funny or radical.[84] And as a woman without a child, I still wonder where the hell Maier gets the money for all the dinners out with friends, how she has time for a fulfilling career *and* leisure, even without kids. Instead, let's reject the *burdens* of child-rearing, the many ways in which our culture and economy are structured to make raising a child into *work*.

Power hints at something fundamentally more relatable to women of all classes and nationalities:

> If, on the other hand, there is something to Maier's regret about having children that is more widely shared than is usually admitted, this would make her negativity something more productive, something that erupts from the centre of the very situation that is supposed to be most comforting and soothing—the familial home, and from the breast of the mother herself, refusing to breastfeed. In a curious way, this notion of queer maternity would . . . present a nihilism not in opposition to, but as part of the very set of "women, domesticity and reproduction."

There are many reasons to regret becoming a mother in a state that makes child-rearing a private social and economic burden for the family and for women especially. Maier's question, "Why wear yourself out for a future that doesn't

---

84   Nina Power, "Motherhood in France: Towards a Queer Maternity?" *Paragraph* 35, no. 2 (2012): 254–64.

include you?" can be asked another way: Why wear yourself out for a *present* that doesn't include you?

But raising a child doesn't have to be, and should not be, treated as an economic burden borne by families or by local public schools in isolation. There is no economic or practical reason why caring for children must be a sacrificial act on the part of mothers or even communities, in isolation. Americans of all ages—whether they are parents or not— must recognize and respect the dignity of children of all backgrounds and classes. Children, like all human beings, *are entitled* to the basic essentials of life. If we can't meet those as society, we have failed as society. When an uninsured child dies of sepsis from a rotted tooth—as happened to twelve-year-old Deamonte Driver in 2007 because his family had lost their Medicaid and could not afford an $80 tooth extraction—we have failed as a society. What happened to Driver's "right to life"? Meanwhile, bestselling parenting books have titles like *Raising Respectful Children in a Disrespectful World* (2013) and *Have the Guts to Do It Right: Raising Grateful and Responsible Children in an Era of Indulgence* (2013).

Just as we can't change schools without changing society, there's little we can do of any significance to change the way middle- and upper-class children are raised without transforming what it means to be a child and care for a child in America. What is the point of bringing up a respectful, loving kid in a free market capitalist society that disrespects the most basic and fundamental rights of its citizens? Are you not simply setting that child up for failure? What is the market value of concern for others? It does not make us more productive.

This is a problem that cannot be addressed in isolation, through self-help or reading the right manuals. It is a systemic problem that requires a structural solution. The care of children must become an economically and emotionally collective experience.

When President Nixon vetoed the Comprehensive Child Development Act, which had been passed by Congress in 1971 and would have mandated federally funded universal child care and early childhood education, he objected—accurately—that it would "commit the vast moral authority of the National Government to the side of communal approaches to child-rearing against the family-centered approach."[85] That is precisely what Americans must demand today.

This harkens back to Shulamith Firestone's *The Dialectic of Sex*,[86] which argued that "sex class" was the original and most invisible form of exploitation and must be overcome by more than just the full integration of women into the labor force. "That so profound a change cannot be easily fitted into traditional categories of thought, e.g., 'political,' is not because these categories do not apply but because they are not big enough: radical feminism bursts through them," writes Firestone. In the book, Firestone makes the strategic decision to accept the dearly held

85 Beatty, *Preschool Education in America*.
86 Shulamith Firestone, *The Dialectic of Sex: The Case for Feminist Revolution* (New York: Farrar, Straus and Giroux, 2003).

notion that women are the biologically weaker sex and proceeds to use it as a basis for advocating for a future in which sex distinction would be undone, and control of the means of reproduction and child care seized by women.[87] This is problematic for many of the reasons second-wave feminism was, but nevertheless, Firestone's critique is astonishing—first, her vision that a revolution in reproductive technology could free women of their biological connection to bearing children, which is as resonant today as it was then; and second, because she is one of a handful of radical feminists to directly confront the conflict that exists between the liberation of women and the liberation of children, because of "mother/child dependency." The oppression of women as the default and unpaid or underpaid caregiver is so intricately bound to the oppression of children, who require some level of guidance and care and are systematically neglected not by their overwhelmed parents, but by a society that asserts it can't "afford" to provide them with a quality education. Firestone's argument rested on contesting the Western perception of children as weak and fragile creatures.

---

87   Like many feminists, I disagree with Firestone in part that the biological family is naturally unequal. Women may lose arm-wrestling competitions with men (without the use of steroids) until the end of time, but weakness is a cultural construct, as anyone who has ever been to a child's cancer ward will understand—it is usually comprised entirely of boys. As adults, men are more vulnerable than women to environment contaminants than women. And aside from the fact that it is painful, the task of giving birth to children need not be seen as a burden. Capitalism causes us to see childbirth and nursing as a waste of our time. However, I am fundamentally in agreement with Firestone about the technological possibilities open to us, were the political economy to change.

A similar strategy was used by some Soviets—who faced the same tension observed by Firestone, out of necessity. As Russian historian Lisa Kirschenbaum observes, "When children appear in accounts of the early years of Soviet power, they often figure as problems that complicated, and perhaps undermined, efforts to liberate women, remake the family, and revolutionize everyday life." Thus,

> by the eve of the Revolution, the Russian kindergarten was animated by a tension between the desire to liberate both women and children and the perceived need to regulate the life of the child and to train women to be modern mothers.[88]

Firestone's ideas about children come largely from historian Philipe Ariès's *Centuries of Childhood* (1962), a profoundly influential work that argued that childhood is a social construction invented after the Middle Ages. For example, Firestone cites Ariès regarding the observations of Louis XIII's doctor, that the Dauphin was able to play violin and sing at eighteen months, entirely uncritically (with no sense that the doctor may be inflating the royal Dauphin) as evidence that children are capable of much more than we imagine. Today, we see Firestone's insistence brought to life as reality for middle-class and upper-class children. In the years since the publication of Ariès's book,

---

88   Lisa A. Kirschenbaum, *Small Comrades: Revolutionizing Childhood in Soviet Russia, 1917–1932* (New York: RoutledgeFalmer, 2000), 9.

historians have countered that Ariès relied too heavily on his interpretation of visual art while ignoring the many diaries, autobiographies, and other artifacts now available, leading him to draw broad and ultimately misleading conclusions about the nature of childhood. Linda Pollock, a historian whose critique rests on a study of hundreds of references to children in the Middle Ages, argues that "the qualitative aspects of care such as protection, love, and socialization are essential for human survival."[89] That is, children are not dolls; certainly they are capable of the same violence, sexuality, love, and complexity that adults are, just in smaller bodies—but nor are they autonomous from the minute they leave the womb.

Ellen Willis has written about meeting up with a fellow second-wave feminist years later and discussing the precariousness of obtaining child care and keeping the household functioning:

The ironies were not lost on us: as feminist activists we, along with the thousands of other young, childless women who dominated the movement, had of course understood that sexual equality required a new system of child-rearing, but the issue remained abstract, unconnected with our most urgent needs; as mothers in the political vacuum of the 80s, along with millions of working parents, we pursue our individual solutions as best

---

89   William A. Corsaro, "Sociology's Rediscovery of Childhood," in *The Sociology of Childhood*, 2nd ed. (Thousand Oaks, CA: Pine Forge Press, 2005).

we can. The political has devolved into the personal, with a vengeance.

Like Pollock and Willis, I believe children need structured guidance to thrive and realize their own self-actualization, and parents need structured child care, just as adults need clean, well-lit spaces to enjoy leisure time. We cannot will unpleasant labor—the "shit work"—away by denying the need for it. Willis met her family's own needs by hiring a nanny that she felt kinship with, while recognizing that this was not a particular solution because it is private. Barbara Ehrenreich and Arlie Russell Hochschild have also pointed out how this individual solution outsources a collective problem onto "third world" countries, with women often leaving their own families and communities behind to immigrate to the United States in exchange for low-paying work, with few rights (since again, it's a labor of love)[90].

That is why we must insist that needs that have been positioned as individual and invisible be made visible and recognized as collective ones. The best way to do this is by making them public. Reconceptualizing the role of the parent from the cultivator of the child, and trusting the child to rely on internal self-directed motivation and free play is transformative for middle-class children who are receiving too much parental intervention—but what about giving working-class children access to some of the joys and privileges of

---

90 Barbara Ehrenreich and Arlie Russell Hochschild, eds., *Global Woman: Nannies, Maids, and Sex Workers in the New Economy* (New York: Holt, 2004).

structured leisure time, like piano lessons? Children do not simply pick up violins and play, of course. They need teachers. Additionally, Firestone's image of working-class children running through the streets and playing on mounds of dirt as "free" is in conflict with her passionate belief in the power of technology and modernity. There are some skills that we need to consciously impart to children to ensure the continuation of a post-industrial modern society, including social skills like cooperation, and educational skills like literacy. The issue is equalizing access to them.

"Society will feed, bring up, and educate the child," writes Firestone. But in a capitalist society, birth control is used as advocated as a way for women to "put off having children until they can afford to." For rich and middle-class women, this means, whenever your employer is ready for you to take leave—note that Google now subsidizes the freezing of eggs for its female employees and calls it feminism. For working-class and poor women, that means never.

This is not an argument against the family, maternal or familial love. It is an argument against the family as the private property of an individual man. Familial love does not need to be confined to the nuclear family; in fact it is often distorted by the unequal economic and social power relations within it. There's a reason why Ella Baker's statement is still so resonant today, "until the killing of black men, black mothers' sons, becomes as important to the rest of the country as the killing of a white mother's sons, we who believe in freedom cannot rest."

In 1967, the Danish journalist Bodil Graae published an

article called "Every Child Should Have a Hundred Parents," a phrase attributed to radical socialist designer Poul Henningsen. Inspired by Henningsen, Graae asked, "What if [children] were welcome to go in and out of the houses, apartments, and homes around us? What if they were accepted among the flowers and as climbers of fences? What if they had the feeling of belonging?"[91] This should be our manifesto.

We should rebel against the imperative to make parents and kids compete for resources and instead use schools as the publicly owned spaces they are and the collaborative spaces they have the power to become, as educator Lisa Delpit writes, by first "acknowledging the inequity of the system," then rejecting or "opting out" of policies like standardized tests, which pit kids against each other in a zero-sum game.

Motherhood may not be radical, but what we call maternal love can be, when extended beyond the nuclear family and beyond the role capitalism has invented for it, as the province of the individual parent/child. Schools can nurture empathetic and critical individuals who are respectful of each other only if teachers welcome and incite students' social critique in the classroom. A teacher's stance should be, according to Delpit,

"Let me show you how to cheat!" and of course to cheat is

91   Bodile Graae, "Born skal have hundrede foraeldre," Politiken, April 9, 1967. Translation by Russell L. Dees, in *Century of the Child: Growing by Design, 1900–2000* by Juliet Kinchin and Aidan O'Connor (MOMA, 2012).

to learn the discourse that would otherwise be used to exclude them from participating in an transforming the mainstream. That is what many Black teachers of the segregated south intended.

We can again let our students know they can resist a system that seeks to limit them to the bottom rung of the social and economic ladder.

To do that, the unequal way we fund schools must change, and the notion of private ownership of children's lives—and women/teachers as primarily accountable for their upbringing—must be eradicated. We must reimagine both the *home* and the *child* as a public, rather than private, space and investment.

That does not mean retreating from society into communes where women take on more of the "shit work." It means demanding economic changes, like a child allowance—in which the state gives direct funds to parents for each child born—and ensuring through organized, democratic means that those changes lead to corresponding and equalizing changes in social relations. Using both the official poverty metric and the supplemental poverty metric, journalists Elizabeth Stoker Bruenig and Matt Bruenig have estimated that implementing a child allowance of $300 a month in replacement of the Earned Income Tax Credit (which costs about $57 billion) would cost $265 billion (in 2012) and cut child poverty rates in half.[92] Further, they say the policy

92   Matt Bruenig, "This One Weird Trick Actually Cuts Child Poverty in Half," *Policy Shop* (blog), Demos, July 21, 2014, demos.org; Matt Bruenig and Elizabeth Stoker, "Republicans and Democrats Both Claim to Be

would "put our national money where our cultural mouth is," by strengthening family. It would also expand our *definition* of "family"—though that change would ultimately require shifts in cultural recognition in addition to redistribution.

A combination of transformations in both recognition and redistribution of funds for the care of children (and adults) is the only way that all men and women who want to share in the occasionally joyful experience of raising a child are able to do so at any time, and women and men who do not want to raise children are still recognized as whole, functioning human beings. As Firestone wrote, "If there were another word more all-embracing than *revolution*—we would use it."[93]

Pro-Family. Here's How They Can Prove It," *New Republic*, April 20, 2014, newrepublic.com.

93   Firestone, *The Dialectic of Sex*.

CONCLUSION:
A CARING SOCIETY

The labour of women and children was, therefore, the first thing sought for by capitalists who used machinery. That mighty substitute for labour and labourers was forthwith changed into a means for increasing the number of wage-labourers by enrolling, under the direct sway of capital, every member of the workman's family, without distinction of age or sex. Compulsory work for the capitalist usurped the place, not only of the children's play, but also of free labour at home within moderate limits for the support of the family.

—*Karl Marx*, Capital

In "I Stand Here Ironing," a story by the American writer and labor organizer Tillie Olsen, we witness a poor unnamed mother addressing her child's teacher through internal monologue. The teacher is a judgmental authority figure who has called that day to arrange a conference. "What you asked me," she says to the teacher, (who, she notes, is "deeply interested in helping" her oldest daughter), "moves tormented back and forth with the iron."

> Even if I came, what good would it do? You think because I am her mother I have a key, or that in some way you could use me as a key? She has lived for nineteen years. There is all that life that has happened outside of me, beyond me. And when is there time to remember, to sift, to weigh, to estimate, to total? I will start and there will be an interruption and I will have to gather it all together again. Or I will become engulfed with all I did or did not do, with what should have been and cannot be helped.[1]

America has long been a land of opportunity and of injustice. Nowhere is the conflict between these twin legacies more apparent than in our efforts to implement universal preschool and reform education. Just as social service workers and some teachers (like the one Olsen's character addresses) scrutinized the morals of working-class mothers as caregivers at the turn of the century, so too do today's business reformers look to "parent education," schools, and especially to teachers, as keys to unlock the potential of each child—operating under the mistaken illusion that once a child has realized his or her

---

1 Tillie Olsen, "I Stand Here Ironing," in *Tell Me a Riddle* (Philadelphia: Lippincott, 1961; New Brunswick, NJ: Rutgers University Press, 1995).

full potential, there's nothing to hold her back from the white-collar careers that politicians and CEOs enthusiastically promise the college-educated.

That does not mean, however, that rising tides lifting all boats is the primary goal of a kinder, friendlier capitalism. Business reformers and the politicians backed by them may call corporate education reform "the civil rights issue of our time," but they are not talking about the rights of students to demand the kind of education that is meaningful to them or the rights of students to take part in broader political struggles. What they are interested in is maintaining the illusion of meritocracy: ensuring all children have, or appear to have, access to the same advantages that middle-class and affluent families ensure their children receive. Thus they attribute social and economic inequality to inequality of opportunity, to the difference between the enrichment class and the after-school program or the violin lesson or the eye-opening trip abroad—and not the entrenched class system of the country, in which there will always be losers, as long as there is a need for wage laborers. Given the extensive evidence that indicates inequality cannot be solved by teachers or schools alone, it takes a particular kind of blindness—the blindness of ideology—to continue to assert that education is the "great equalizer." To the extent that the public schools reinforce this belief, they are instrumental in the perpetuation of class inequality.

The difference in ideological approaches to understanding education between conservatives and liberals is substantive, but ultimately immaterial. Conservatives frame the crisis of child poverty as one that the poor have brought on themselves through laziness, and argue the "achievement gap" between Black and white children can be chalked up to genetic differences. Richard Herrnstein and Charles Murray's *The Bell Curve*[2] is the essential text for this theory, which falls apart easily when we consider that the income achievement gap is now twice the size of the achievement gap between Black and white students, and growing (and that the Black-white achievement gap has narrowed any time there has been a concerted campaign to integrate public schools).[3]

Liberals, on the other hand, see poverty as the natural consequence of a lack of access to resources, identifying, for example, exposure to books and words at an early age, or to effective teachers, as a panacea to solve the problems of educational equity.

It was not inevitable that it would be the schools over which the major battles of the Civil Rights Movement were fought. After all, Martin Luther King Jr. not only dreamed that the children of "Black men and white men, Jews and Gentiles, Protestants and Catholics," would one day join hands and sing "Free at Last"—he also asserted that "no work is insignificant," that "All labor that uplifts humanity has dignity and importance."

---

2   Richard J. Herrnstein and Charles A. Murray, *The Bell Curve: Intelligence and Class Structure in American Life* (New York: Free Press, 1994).

3   Sean F. Reardon, "The Widening Academic Achievement Gap Between the Rich and the Poor: New Evidence and Possible Explanations," in *Whither Opportunity?: Rising Inequality, Schools, and Children's Life Chances*, eds. Greg J. Duncan and Richard J. Murnane (New York: Russell Sage Foundation, 2011), cepa.stanford.edu.

It's difficult, given the weakness of the labor movement and the political left in the past three decades, for those of us under fifty to look back on the federal government's forced integration of the public schools in the 1960s and 70s as anything but radical; however, it is critical to remember that busing students to schools in different neighborhoods as a way to achieve racial and socioeconomic diversity was based on fundamentally meritocratic assumptions about redistribution. It was a strategy that appealed to the politically palatable desire to give opportunites to "needy children," rather than to redistribute resources to poor adults. It came from a place of tolerance rather than justice. And its unpopularity—mostly among whites, but among some Black families as well—helped sow the seeds of the reactionary politics of the 1980s, without the benefit of permanently and fundamentally reshaping society, as a broader redistributive project might have. In fact, just a few decades later, as I've described, many of the advances of integration during the 1960s and 70s have been undone.

Yet, it is this tradition, not King's demand for dignified work, that President Obama and Secretary of Education Arne Duncan have chosen to resurrect from the past as they renew the push for Universal Pre-K: "We know that right now during the first three years of life, a child born into a low-income family hears 30 million fewer words than a child born into a well-off family," Obama said in June 2013, echoing the exact same research about the "30 million word gap" by age three, or cognitive deficits in low-income children who hear fewer words at home, documented by the same

researchers (Betty Hart and Todd Risley) who influenced the
development of Head Start decades prior.[4]

> By giving more of our kids access to high-quality
> preschool and other early learning programs, and by help-
> ing parents get the tools they need to help their kids
> succeed, we can give those kids a better shot at the career
> they are capable of, and a life that will make us all better
> off.[5]

Yes—we should equalize the distribution of educational
resources among children of all classes, but what happens
when they grow up into adults? Will they actually have a
"shot at the career they are capable of?" As Jean Anyon
and others have pointed out time and again, the fulfilling
career in computer science is not a guarantee, even if you
know how to code: There are simply far more qualified
graduates than there are jobs that pay living wages in
America.[6] And, in their important book *Schooling in
Capitalist America*, Marxist sociologists Samuel Bowles and
Herbert Gintis argue, based on extensive research, that,
"social class or racial differences in IQ are nearly irrelevant to the process of intergenerational status

4   Betty Hart and Todd R. Risley, "The Early Catastrophe: The 30
Million Word Gap by Age 3," *American Educator* 27, no. 1 (Spring 2003):
4–9, summary by Rice University School Literacy and Culture at literacy.
rice.edu.
5   White House Initiative on Educational Excellence for Hispanics, U.S.
Department of Education, "Bridging the Word Gap," ed.gov.
6   Jean Anyon, *Radical Possibilities: Public Policy, Urban Education, and
a New Social Movement* (New York: Routledge, 2005).

transmission." This is a strong critique of well-meaning liberal projects to make society more equal by increasing access to educational opportunity in order to compensate for disparities in resources in the upbringing of poor and working-class versus middle-class or wealthy children.[7]

Children don't live in a vacuum. They don't grow up or graduate into a world separate from their parents or caregivers. A child whose parent—beloved, admired, or flawed—is sitting in a jail cell, or exhausting him- or herself in multiple low-wage jobs, will never have access to the same educational experience as a child whose parent is free. Likewise, schools do not exist in a vacuum. They don't create inequality, but neither will the mere existence of a free universal public school system—even one that extends into early childhood—cure it. A society that puts its money where its mouth is and expresses genuine concern for the well-being of its children, will ensure that every adult as well as every child has access to the essentials required to live—starting with quality health care, nutritious meals, and leisure time. The best system for translating this ideal into a material reality is likely a universal basic income that follows the child throughout her life, guaranteeing a basic standard of living, as well as a more equal distribution of income and work.

A 2013 paper by economists calculated the cost of a universal basic child income system awarding parents fifty euros per child per month across the European Union at 0.15 percent of

---

7   Samuel Bowles and Herbert Gintis, *Schooling in Capitalist America: Educational Reform and the Contradictions of Economic Life* (New York: Basic Books, 1976).

EU GDP. Using a tax-benefit microsimulation model, the authors of the paper estimated that the benefit, which could be funded by an EU flat tax of 0.2 percent and complemented with a national tax as needed, would reduce the risk of child poverty by 14 percent. This is a start, but not nearly enough, especially given the uniquely large and appalling divide in resources—educational and otherwise—between white children and children of color, as well as rich children and poor children, in America. To equalize the disparity and pay back the "education debt" owed will frankly require demanding that the top 1 percent of earners give back some of the dramatic increases in wealth they've accumulated during the recession, through a targeted tax increase on the highest earners.[8] Another source of funding is requiring corporations to make good on their outstanding tax obligations—and requiring, as New York has done, states to pay back what they owe for years of underfunding of schools in poor cities, districts, and neighborhoods. In 2006, the Campaign for Fiscal Equity won a landmark lawsuit ruling that New York state had violated students' constitutional right to a sound, basic education, and was thus required to pay back over $5.9 billion to schools "in the next few years." New York City is owed 47 percent of the funds.[9] The major New York

---

8   Horacio Levy, Manos Matsaganis, and Holly Sutherland, "Towards a European Union Child Basic Income?: Within and Between Country Effects," *International Journal of Microsimulation* 6, no. 1 (2013): 63–85, microsimulation.org.

9   Marina Marcon-O'Malley, "Billions Behind: New York State Continues to Violate Students' Constitutional Rights," Alliance for Quality Education, 2014; Eliza Shapiro, "Report: State Still Owes Its Schools $5.9 Billion," *Capital*, August 7, 2014, capitalnewyork.com.

teachers' union, the United Federation of Teachers (UFT) and the Alliance for Quality Education (AQE, a major education advocacy group) along with NYC Mayor Bill de Blasio and Syracuse Mayor Stephanie Miner have come together to publicize the verdict. The UFT and AQE launched a website, howmuchnysrobbed.nyc, which allows users to search a school by school name or district and determine the exact amount that school is owed by the state.

Still, the question remains: Who, as radical feminist Ellen Willis put it in a diary entry, "will do the shit work?"[10] Because there are only so many hours in the day, the current standardized eight-hour workday and forty-hour workweek assume the existence of a stay-at-home wife and mother or else, a nanny and housekeeper, to perform child care and chores. In American free-market capitalism, those services are provided "for free" by mothers and wives, or by hired help, including concierge services as well as nannies and housekeepers. Every time a parent gives birth or adopts a child, she has chosen to sacrifice some of her limited time or money. Mothers, especially poor ones, presently work longer hours than anyone else in the economy. Despite their instrumental status in ensuring the economy continues, care workers including teachers and paraprofessionals, home health aides, and nurses are dramatically underpaid. Modern families scrape together their own individualized solutions, often based on some combination of these, or living in a

---

10 Ellen Willis and Spencer Ackerman, "Up From Radicalism: A Feminist Journal," in *The Essential Ellen Willis*, ed. Nona Willis Aronowitz (Minneapolis, MN: University of Minnesota Press, 2014).

dirtier home than they'd like. A society built around care rather than profit would prioritize the provision of basic goods and services for all. In a caring society that values child-rearing as well as the caretaking of the ill and elderly, all care workers, whether they are working jobs considered "professional" or not, would be paid high salaries. There would be no need to, as a *Jezebel* article recently put it, "Talk about Women Who Regret Motherhood," because there would either be no regret (if the reason is financial or related to the difficulty and isolation of individual child-rearing), or no stigma involved in giving a child up for adoption.[11] Again, for the structure of the preschool or K–12 school to change, the structure of the workplace would have to change, since children and adults do not live parallel lives.

I am always struck by teachers and administrators who sigh when parents sign up their children for after-school programs or, in preschool, "extended hour." I frequently hear teachers say, sadly, "Eight hours is a long day for a kid." It is also a long day for an adult. And increasingly long workdays for professionals mean even longer workdays for child-care workers and others in the service industry, like those who deliver groceries, to support them. Work that is not always pleasant—the classic example is collecting garbage, but this also applies to some aspects of raising children, like changing diapers, or listening to the tenth, mind-numbing rendition of the ABC song in one day—will be necessary to

11   Tracy Moore, "We Need to Talk about Women Who Regret Motherhood," *Jezebel*, September 18, 2014, jezebel.com.

perform for the foreseeable future in order to maintain the modern standard of living. Such work may not be immediately enjoyable, but it is immensely meaningful: It is critical to our collective survival. There is no reason why these tasks must be done individually, by those of low socioeconomic status. Instead the burden should be fairly distributed among all members of society.

What would we do all day?

What will "school" look like, and what will we mean by "work," in a society liberated from the profit imperatives of capitalism?

One of the central problems in imagining a system of education for liberation is the perceived tension between freedom and discipline. Should educators who seek to change society aim to inculcate a specific set of values in students, or trust that students will arrive at a critical analysis of society by experiencing education as equal participants in their learning process, allowed to arrive at their own conclusions rather than follow a prescribed ideological path? Often, this is framed as a question of whether indoctrination can coexist with democratic process. In 1973, Bobby Seale asserted, "We're not here to teach our children what to think. We're here to teach our children how to think!"

Historian Daniel Perlstein has contrasted the pedagogy of the Student Nonviolent Coordinating Committee (SNCC) freedom schools—largely representative of a grassroots educational experience started from the ground

up and constructed by a real community, with the philosophy behind Black Panther schools. After the Watts "riot" of
1965, he observes, activists like James Garrett, founder of
the Black Student Union at San Francisco State University,
abandoned the progressive pedagogy practiced by SNCC,
which "trusted students to discover the truth." Students
were instead "informed" about culture and politics.[12] The
Black Panther's 1966 educational program had as its primary
goal the transmission of party ideology and explicit instruction about class struggle. "A commitment to transmitting
their revolutionary analysis led the Panthers to use a banking language in their educational proposals," Perlstein
concludes. (Banking language refers to the idea that
students' minds are empty receptacles to be filled with a
teacher's knowledge.) "Whereas SNCC had once embraced
a pedagogy of open-ended inquiry, the Panthers applauded
explicit, direct instruction in revolutionary analysis." For
example, in the first Panther school, opened in 1969, students
marched in military uniforms and sang songs about greedy
pigs exploiting people of all colors all over the world.
Ultimately, Perlstein sees SNCC schools as reformist—
using an education based in liberal, rather than leftist,
values of self-actualization in place of a broader political
analysis—and Panther ideology as revolutionary. He notes
that as women played an increasingly prominent role in the

---

12 Daniel Perlstein, "Freedom, Liberation, Accommodation: Politics
and Pedagogy in SNCC and the Black Panther Party," in *Teach Freedom:
Education for Liberation in the African-American Tradition,* ed. Charles M.
Payne and Carol Sills Strickland (New York: Teachers College Press, 2008).

party, the pedagogical approach changed again to become more student-centered (which he sees as a sign of the abandonment of activism).

SNCC freedom school teacher Fannie Theresa Rushing has responded to Perlstein's history, that,

> The objectives of the Freedom School and the pedagogy of Paulo Freire were to be transformative social change agents. They were not predicated, as the article seems to indicate, on individual self-validation. Looking within one's self for the ability to eradicate oppression is only the first step, not an end in itself . . . one of the objectives of the Freedom School was the improvement of life chances not just for the individual, but for the group.[13]

In other words, students were taught that the personal is political, as the feminist saying goes, but that the goal of education should be not just the lifting of the individual—which can only lead to tokenization—but the changing of circumstances and political possibilities of all oppressed and working-class people. Perlstein's dichotomy between self-directed learning, and the passing down and absorption of collective history is a common one, but it's false. Education should be a balance between the two modes. Rushing does not see a conflict between teaching these skills and the ambition to recognize and fight structural oppression. Children

---

13 Fannie Theresa Rushing, "Minds Still Stayed on Freedom?: Reflections on Politics, Consensus, and Pedagogy in the African American Freedom Struggle," in Payne and Strickland, *Teach Freedom.*

must learn how to think, in Seale's words, but there is no way to do that without influencing them politically.[14]

All education is to some extent character education. Educators who believe they can be objective in the classroom or who have fantasies of letting young children make every decision for themselves, end up giving up the chance to really be present themselves. On the other hand, who decides what the proper focus of education is?

The meaning of practice: collective reflection and action. As most everyone who has been up at the blackboard, whiteboard, or smartboard wondering how to meaningfully fill an hour understands, teachers model more than the effective use of the writing process or how to punctuate a sentence. Teachers are examples of how to learn, how to *be*.

What matters is that students and adults are involved together in work that is meaningful to them.

And here, again, I couldn't disagree more with French mom and sensational author Corinne Maier that "in the Land of Merchandise, the child is in its element. It's great for capitalism—always more things, always more crap you can't recycle, interchangeable junk soon forgotten and endlessly replaceable . . . that is exactly what the child wants." Baby registries are the creation of adults who want to make their kids look cute. All that junk isn't bought by kids; it's bought

---

14   Charles E. Jones and Jonathan Gayles have described how the Intercommunal Youth Institute (IYI) successfully tied progressive pedagogy to radical politics by conceptualizing "the world as a child's classroom." Charles E. Jones and Jonathan Gayles, "'The World Is a Child's Classroom': An Analysis of the Black Panther Party's Oakland Community School," in Payne and Strickland, *Teach Freedom*.

by rushed parents who are too guilty or who don't have the time to say "no" to their children.[15] Kids are naturally curious, but they are as happy with a stack of differently shaped leaves or a basin full of soapy water as they are with a Barbie doll.

In preschool, no matter how independent they are, children are eager to wash the table after lunch or feed the fish or sweep up the floor. It is not because they are stupid or naïve or need constant positive reinforcement and attention. It's because they rightfully perceive that these tasks are *important*, essential to the functioning of the classroom for the group. In public schools and charter schools where the teacher feels a personal need or pressure from administrators to be constantly, vigilantly "managing behavior," with "no excuses" for minor infractions, students' sense of ownership and control over their own learning and environment is destroyed and sometimes humiliated out of them. What else is the point of having them switch classrooms seven or eight or ten times a day? Just as they are becoming comfortable in a room, a bill rings and they must anxiously hurry to their next class, or face a lateness penalty. No wonder by high school they don't care whether they get there on time or not. No one wins.

Children of all ages are acutely aware of their own powerlessness within schools and society as it is currently structured. For example, every year, during the first few months

15   Corinne Maier, *No Kids: 40 Good Reasons Not to Have Children*, trans. Patrick Watson (Toronto: McClelland & Stewart, 2009).

of school, the two-year-olds in the toddler classroom at the preschool where I work discover that by banging their cups on the table together, they can make a loud, demanding noise and provoke a reaction from teachers, a thrilling proposition for someone who is used to mostly being acted upon. And as cliché as it sounds, in my experience as a high school teacher, when I stopped trying to "manage the classroom" and started relating to my students with the same respect, directness, honesty, and overt friendliness that I would any other coworker, I stopped having class-wide behavioral problems.

This is perhaps why students are so frequently at the forefront of movements for social change. In the fall of 2014, I interviewed Brian Jones, a former New York City elementary school teacher and candidate for New York lieutenant governor, and current education activist and PhD student in urban education at City University of New York. Jones is writing his dissertation on student struggles in Tuskegee and Alabama in 1968. When I asked him what lessons movements to seize control of education today can take from the past, he responded,

> I've noticed there's a pattern in moments of dramatic social change when people are trying to change circumstances, especially when they do it in huge numbers— invariably, if you go to any spot on the globe where that's going on and turn your attention to the schools, young people in the schools are insisting on dramatically transforming their education . . . You could just go anywhere in the world and look at what young people demand in

moments of social upheaval. It's always been that they want to have more power and control over what it is they learned and they want to be able to work together and do things that are intrinsically worth doing. Not artificial school.

He cites the American South under Jim Crow laws mandating racial segregation as a prime example: Students "sit down in these classrooms and say, well, this is intolerable—how can they sit here like this? How do you teachers talk to us at a time like this? This needs to change." Self-motivated collective education is the most powerful education, says Jones.

For parents and teachers, this means standing with students instead of against them. Corporate reformers have made a critical strategic mistake in closing "under-resourced" or "failing" schools in cities around the country, like Chicago and New York. Never before have parents, teachers, and students been so united across race and class lines in defending their local schools. Never has the possibility for a movement been greater. In New York City, UFT chapter leader Julie Cavanagh—who participated in a lawsuit against Mayor Bloomberg for the right to protest school closings and charter schools—seeks to replicate the success of CORE, the Caucus of Rank and File Educators in Chicago, with MORE, the Movement of Rank and File Educators, an explicitly social justice caucus.

Building a lasting opposition to the neoliberal consensus on education "reform" will require teachers unions to form broad, international alliances with the general public, instead of bargaining for seniority provisions and miniscule pay raises that never come as promised. Teachers must focus their advocacy on actions that clearly benefit students as much as they benefit teachers. That means speaking up when it comes to issues that affect the lives of their students—high-stakes testing, yes, but also the deepening of segregation in our schools; police brutality in schools and communities; the lack of access for low-income families to health care; and the US prison state, which disproportionately affects low-income and Black students. That's what it means to put students first.

Beyond organizing for political change, there is, of course, the future to imagine: the possibility of schools to be a place where adults and children play and learn together. Instead of shaping children into the image of adults through the "work" of school, adults should be attentive to, as groups advocating for societal change from the Soviet revolutionaries to the Panthers have been, the amazing symbolic meaning of child-hood, and actual new ideas that might be considered "utopian." Critically, in the words (again) of Freire,

> Education either functions as an instrument which is used to facilitate integration of the younger generation into the logic of the present system and bring about conformity, or it becomes the practice of freedom, the means by which men and women deal critically and creatively with reality and discover how to participate in the transformation of their world.[16]

---

16   Paulo Freire, *Pedagogy of the Oppressed* (New York: Bloomsbury, 2000).

The preschools in Reggio Emilia, a small city in northern Italy, are a fascinating example of what a school system that helps people deal critically and creatively with their world might look like. They are consistently rated among the best schools in the world and recognized by the OECD and educational institutions as a point of reference and inspiration. That the city itself is considered one of the most livable in Italy for offering high-quality social services and horizontal relationships for citizens, and that it commits over 14 percent of the city budget to early childhood, illustrates the extent to which visions for schools and visions for society overlap. They were founded in the aftermath of World War II, which reduced infrastructure to rubble, by a group of parents, "women, men, young people—all farmers and workers, all special people who had survived a hundred war horrors" who put up money and located a building cooperatively. Loris Malaguzzi, one of the original founders, remembers:

I felt a pact, an alliance, with children, adults, veterans from prison camps, partisans of the Resistance, and the sufferers of a devastated world. Yet all that suffering was pushed away by a day in spring, when ideas and feelings turned toward the future seemed so much stronger than those that called on to halt and focus on the present.[17]

17   Carolyn Edwards, Lella Gandini, and George Forman, eds., *The Hundred Languages of Children: The Reggio Emilia Experience in Transformation*, 3rd ed. (Santa Barbara, CA: Praeger, 2011).

When women began taking jobs in civic society in large numbers in Italy in the 1960s, demand for the schools grew rapidly, and in 1967, parent-run schools came under the administration of the municipality. Reggio Emilia schools are known for the beauty of the environment—using natural and recycled materials like stone, water, wood, plants, and light in interesting ways—and the beauty of children's artwork. Children work on long-term projects that arise based on their own questions about the world. Malaguzzi reflects:

> In such a time as this, with a society and culture that tend to isolate, to give young children the possibility of being together for several years and working closely together is like an emergency life raft. Their relationships are really something new and different from the close relationships that are inside the family or the usual peer relationships in traditional schools. These new cooperative relationships among young children have not yet been sufficiently studied in terms of their educational potential. They offer children the opportunity to realize that their ideas are different and that they hold a unique point of view. At the same time, children realize that the world is multiple and that other children can be discovered through a negotiation of ideas. Instead of interacting only through feelings and sense of friendship, they discover how satisfying it is to exchange ideas and thereby transform their environment.

That is, as Fannie Rushing pointed out,[18] respectful and democratic relationships between teachers and students and students as peers can give children the power to relate to the group as a whole, and understand themselves as actors in shaping and reshaping the world.

Recently, I came across a line from Virginia Woolf's *The Years* quoted in a book review by Jacqueline Rose. The book, which follows several members of one family on single days over the course of many years, was written on the eve of World War II, which must have influenced Woolf's comment on parental possessiveness.

> Oh Lord, North said to himself, she's as bad as they are. She was glazed; insincere. They were talking about her children now . . . *My* boy—*my* girl . . . they were saying. But they're not interested in other people's children, he observed. Only in their own; their own property; their own flesh and blood, which they would protect with the unsheathed claws for the primeval swamp, he thought . . . how then can we be civilized?[19]

"Maternal" feeling as it is constructed in a sexist and capitalist society is inhumane, because "other people's children" are abstract generalizations that occupy the lives and minds of others—unlike our own children, who absorb us completely. But this conception of motherhood, childhood,

---

18 Rushing, "Minds Still Stayed on Freedom?"
19 Jacqueline Rose, "Mothers," *London Review of Books* 36, no. 12, June 19, 2014: 17–22.

and indeed, humanity as isolated and separate is not any more natural than wage labor, or the forty-hour workweek.

In a society in which people are invested in the survival of others, caregivers would actively take an interest in "other people's children." I spend all day for most of the week with children who are not my own, and I grow to love them. They are all special, with their own specific voices and ways of speaking—not as the consumerist grotesques painted by Maier and others, or as the wimpy individualists who need a trophy for every accomplishment, as they are painted by conservatives—but because they're alive and human and prone, like me or anyone, to suffering. That is why human beings continue to have children, even by choice, despite its deep impracticality in free-market American society. What better platform to organize a movement around? And who better than teachers and caregivers to lead us into a world where every child is valued collectively and equally, for who she is, not what she can prove she can do—in outright defiance of the logic of capitalism?